Rachel Macy Stafford's post "The Day I Stopped Saying Hurry Up" was a true phenomenon on the *Huffington Post*, igniting countless conversations online and off about freeing ourselves from the vicious cycle of keeping up with our overstuffed agendas. *Hands Free Mama* has the power to keep that conversation going and remind us that we must not let our lives pass us by.

> Arianna Huffington, chair, president, and editor-in-chief of the Huffington Post Media Group, nationally syndicated columnist, and author of thirteen books; *huffingtonpost.com*

With deeply personal stories and inspiring tips, this book offers a much-needed reminder to let go of daily distractions and grasp what matters most in life. Stafford's anecdotes resonate with me, as it is also my hope to cherish the present moment with family and loved ones.

> Randi Zuckerberg, former Facebook marketing executive and current CEO/founder of Zuckerberg Media

The truth is, I was afraid to read this book, because I don't want to put down my phone. I wasn't sure I wanted to know the things that Rachel had to teach me. I'm so glad I didn't let my resistance to change keep me from reading this visionary book. Rachel is a rare mix of wisdom and gentleness. She doesn't preach—she just gently reminds us of what we used to know about joy but forgot, and that's what makes Rachel such a relevant, brilliant, important voice. She gently calls us back to what we used to know. It's impossible to read this book without experiencing tidal waves of gratitude and peace. Rachel's book is a gift.

> Glennon Doyle Melton, author of the *New York Times* bestseller *Carry On, Warrior*, and founder of *Momastery.com*

Distraction is killing us—our relationships with ourselves and with others. I love this book for slowing me down and helping me see again what is most important.

> Patti Digh, author of *Life Is a Verb*

In our quest to be perfect, organized, readily available, and committed to juggling a million different things at once, *Hands Free Mama* offers stories, anecdotes, tips, and thoughtful advice about dealing with daily distractions and learning how to recognize what is truly important in life. Rachel's writing and passion on the subject are unmatched. I relate in some way to every story. Highly recommended!

> Amy McCready, founder of Positive Parenting Solutions and author of *If I Have to Tell You One More Time . . . The Revolutionary Program That Gets Your Kids to Listen Without Nagging, Reminding or Yelling*

Whether you're a stressed parent who can't seem to make time for all the "must-dos" and still focus on what matters, or you simply want to learn to live more presently in our high-tech culture, *Ha⋯⋯⋯⋯⋯⋯⋯⋯⋯⋯⋯* ey and wisdom will help you learn to app⋯⋯⋯⋯⋯⋯⋯⋯ e.

> Meagan Francis, ⋯⋯⋯⋯⋯⋯⋯⋯ to *Enjoying Mothe⋯⋯⋯⋯⋯⋯⋯* m

Rachel's gentle words of encouragement and practical ideas come to me again and again as I go about my day and make me a better parent and person. I so appreciate her intentional approach to parenting and focusing on what's most important.

Ali Edwards, memory-keeping blogger, instructor, and author of *Life Artist*

I was moved to tears by this beautiful book. *Hands Free Mama* is true inspiration for parents to slow down and behold the miracle of childhood before it slips away.

Harley A. Rotbart, M.D., Professor and Vice Chair of Pediatrics, University of Colorado, author of *No Regrets Parenting: Turning Long Days and Short Years into Cherished Moments with Your Kids*

I don't think it is possible to read this book without changing your relationship to media and to your family. Rachel offers wisdom, guidance, love, and support to move to a *Hands Free* life. From the first chapter I felt both inspired and empowered to disconnect from my devices and reconnect with my family. This is a must read for every parent!

Darci Walker, PsyD.

This volume is a gift to every new mother and to every seasoned veteran who has ever "plugged in." Look up. Be present. Don't miss it. Rachel Stafford shows you how.

Elizabeth Foss, author, *Small Steps for Catholic Moms*; *elizabethfoss.com*

This isn't a book, it's a movement; a wakeup call with instructions on how not to miss a childhood. A priceless gift.

Samantha Ettus, bestselling author and lifestyle and parenting expert for working women

If you are struggling with putting that new shiny iPhone away, this book is for you! I hope that you will join the Hands Free Mama revolution and challenge yourself and your family to do the same. It'll change your life.

Pam Moore, founder and CEO of digital agency Marketing Nutz and a Forbes Top 10 Social Media Power Influencer

HANDS FREE Mama

A GUIDE TO PUTTING DOWN the PHONE, BURNING the TO-DO LIST, and LETTING GO of PERFECTION to GRASP WHAT REALLY MATTERS!

Rachel Macy Stafford

ZONDERVAN®

ZONDERVAN

Hands Free Mama
Copyright © 2013 by Rachel Macy Stafford

This title is also available as a Zondervan ebook. Visit www.zondervan.com/ebooks.

Requests for information should be addressed to:

Zondervan, *Grand Rapids, Michigan* 49530

Library of Congress Cataloging-in-Publication Data

Stafford, Rachel Macy, 1972-
    Hands free mama : a guide to putting down the phone, burning the to-do list,
and letting go of perfection to grasp what really matters! / Rachel Macy Stafford.
      pages cm
      ISBN 978-0-310-33813-0 (softcover)
      1. Parenting. 2. Parent and child. 3. distraction (Psychology) 4. Values.
5. Parenting—Religious aspects—Christianity. I. Title.
HQ755.8.S7186 2013
   306.874—dc23   2013026572

Any Internet addresses (websites, blogs, etc.) and telephone numbers in this book are
offered as a resource. They are not intended in any way to be or imply an endorsement
by Zondervan, nor does Zondervan vouch for the content of these sites and numbers
for the life of this book.

The author is represented by MacGregor Literary, Inc., of Hillsboro, Oregon.

Cover design: Juice Box Designs
Interior design: Matthew Van Zomeren

Printed in the United States of America

---

17 18 19 20 21 22 /DCI/ 20 19 18 17 16 15 14 13 12

For Natalie and Avery—
because without you, there would be no stories

CONTENTS

INTRODUCTION: WHY HANDS FREE?

I KEPT TELLING MYSELF things would eventually slow down. *Someday.* Who was I kidding?

That two-year period of my highly distracted life was a blur. There aren't too many moments—good or bad—I can recollect from that time, but I'll never forget this one.

I'd just arrived home from a community event I'd spent hundreds of volunteer hours planning. Although I knew my husband was about to tuck my kids into bed, I couldn't join him. Instead, I collapsed on my own bed fully clothed. Sitting mere inches away on the bedside table was the substance of my life: a typed to-do list, a buzzing phone, a laptop computer, and a bulging daily planner. Every day, that stack of papers and duo of devices captured my heart, my focus, and my energy.

My smartphone's flashing red light served as a tormenting reminder that none of these distractions were going anywhere. Information overload, electronic gadgets, packed schedules, and unachievable standards would all be waiting for me tomorrow—and the day after that and the day after that. *Someday* was merely a word I used to avoid facing the frenzied reality that had become my life.

Someday, I told myself, *there will be a healthy amount of white space in my monthly planner. Someday, my daily agenda will be determined by my heart's desire, not by tweets, beeps, and dings. Someday, I'll say no to heading up bake sales and book fairs and the quest for spotless counters and perfectly styled hair. Someday, I'll say yes to puddle jumping in the rain, disheveled ponytails, and extra bedtime stories. Someday, I'll look into my children's eyes and hear every syllable of their tender, silly words. Someday, I'll close my laptop and kiss my spouse before he walks out the door. Someday, I'll remember what it feels like to laugh, play, relax, and enjoy life. Someday, I'll have time for what truly matters.*

A life of simple pleasures was an elusive dream that, at full-throttle speed, I could not grasp. Each time I told my children, "Not now, Mom's busy," my chance for a meaningful, joy-filled life edged farther away. Even in that exhausted moment on my bed, as my children slipped into pajamas and chose bedtime stories just one floor above, a peaceful existence seemed little more than a fantasy.

As I lay there, too drained to cry and too ashamed to ask for help, I realized just how bad my condition was. I was buried — buried beneath the weight of my distractions. I was no longer living. I was just barely existing.

I knew I'd come to a crossroads. I could continue my distracted ways, separating myself farther from my idyllic *someday* existence, or I could start digging — digging for air, for hope, for life.

I chose to dig.

Because someday is nowhere to live your life.

That undeniable truth hit me hard during a morning run shortly after I acknowledged my buried state. The realization was so painful that it caused a physical reaction that literally brought me to my knees. For the first time, I honestly answered the question that for years had given me a great deal of pride: How *do* I do it all?

I miss out on life — that's how I do it all. I miss out on what truly matters; and what I miss, I can't get back.

This breakdown-breakthrough moment propelled me into my life-changing Hands Free journey. In that moment, I looked to

God for help. I've felt his presence throughout my life, particularly in my work as a special-education teacher and in my writing, but this was different. I knew I couldn't overcome my distracted ways without his guidance and strength. With a renewed spirit, I began implementing simple strategies that enabled me to let go of my daily distractions and grasp moments of loving connection.

With each step, I grew increasingly free of my buried state. Through every touch of my child's hand, every meaningful conversation with my spouse, every glimpse of the beautiful world I had been too busy to notice, the addictive grip of distraction began to loosen. Over time these efforts proved powerful enough to transform my distracted life into one of meaningful fulfillment and connection. I was no longer putting off life until *someday*. For the first time in a long time I invested my time, focus, energy, and love in *today*. And that's when I discovered the power of living Hands Free.

THE HANDS FREE REVOLUTION

Change begins with a spark of recognition within one's heart. And when this newfound awareness is shared, this spark has the potential to spread. That is what happened when I started blogging about my daily struggles and triumphs toward a less distracted life. Using my passions for teaching, writing, and encouraging others, I shared my attempts to live joyfully and presently in a fast-paced, overly pressured, media-saturated world.

As stories from my journey fell into the hands (and onto the screens) of others who also felt trapped by their distractions, I suddenly had companions on my Hands Free journey. As a means of providing my readers with tips on unplugging and connecting to loved ones, I created *The Hands Free Revolution* Facebook page. Little did I know it would become more than a page, but an entire movement for mindful technology use and grasping the moments that matter. A community of people who were determined to reject societal pressures to live a hurried, fractured, and disconnected existence grew organically. *The Hands Free Revolution* quickly became more than a community of like-minded people; it became the means to a more meaningfully connected life.

When members of *The Hands Free Revolution* began sharing their stories and experiences, I discovered it wasn't just stressed-out moms who were struggling. I heard from a Fortune 500 company executive, a stay-at-home dad, a single mom living in a battered-women's shelter, a homeschooler, a grandmother, a blogger, and a teen — all of whom were implementing Hands Free strategies and experiencing the life-altering results. That is when I realized *anyone* can become a Hands Free Mama. Anyone who feels buried, regardless of background or circumstances, can let go of distraction and grasp what really matters. If there is hope for me, there is hope for anyone. The pathway to a Hands Free life is accessible to all and begins with a single step.

BECOMING HANDS FREE

The chapters of this book reflect the step-by-step progression of my journey to a less distracted life. The twelve chapters encompass the letting-go actions I used to break free from distraction and live a more present and fulfilling life. Each chapter contains stories from my journey that illuminate steps in the transformation. After each story, you will find a weekly "Hands Free Intention" section, which offers a practical way to incorporate each letting-go action into your life. At the end of every chapter, a "Hands Free Reflection" encourages introspection as you move forward in your journey. These short passages can be used as a meditation, prayer, mantra, or reminder as you reflect on the themes of each chapter.

The book is formatted for a yearlong transformation, one chapter a month, although your journey may well take on a life of its own. You may proceed faster or slower. You may decide to begin journaling as a means of deepening your experience. You may embark on this journey with a friend, a family member, or a small group to provide support and accountability. Feel free to work through the book in the manner that most benefits you, your family, and your circumstances. My hope is that this book will be become lovingly worn with dog-eared pages and coffee stains, that it will not be just a one-time read, but a reference for daily focus and resolve. May this book be your tool to start digging—digging for the life you want to live *now*, not *someday*. May letting go to grasp what really matters soon become the practice of your life as it is for mine.

I must tell you, however, that my house is not what it used to be; my social calendar is not what it used to be; my filing system is not what it used to be; my daily agenda is not what it used to be; my gold-star supermom status is not what it used to be. I am not what I used to be. I am now living life with open eyes, open heart, and open hands—and I never want to go back!

My friend, there is life to be lived. There is hope to be found. There are moments to grasp. Come on—take my hand. After being tied up for so long, it's finally free.

Rachel

THE HANDS FREE PLEDGE

I'm becoming Hands Free.

I want to make memories, not to-do lists.

I want to feel the squeeze of my child's arms, not the pressure of overcommitment.

I want to get lost in conversation with the people I love, not consumed by a sea of unimportant emails.

I want to be overwhelmed by sunsets that give me hope, not by overloaded agendas that steal my joy.

I want the noise of my life to be a mixture of laughter and gratitude, not the intrusive buzz of cell phones and text messages.

I'm letting go of distraction, disconnection, and perfection to live a life that simply, so very simply, consists of what really matters.

I'm becoming Hands Free.

Chapter 1

ACKNOWLEDGE THE COST OF YOUR DISTRACTION

Awareness

One of the most tragic things I know about human nature is that all of us tend to put off living. We are all dreaming of some magical rose garden over the horizon — instead of enjoying the roses that are blooming outside our windows today.

Dale Carnegie

MAYBE IT WAS THE RECURRING DISAPPOINTMENT in my children's faces when I told them I didn't have time. Maybe it was the superficial hellos and hasty goodbyes offered to my spouse. Maybe it was the persistent feeling of unease — like I was missing something important. Maybe it was a combination of all these troubling factors that finally made me ask, *Is this really how I want to live?*

The first and most critical step in this journey is gaining awareness. I had to acknowledge all the precious moments I was missing and would continue to miss as a result of my distracted ways. Taking this difficult look inward was a prerequisite to beginning my transformation. If I hadn't first made an assessment of the irreparable damage caused by my tech-obsessed, multitasking ways, even my most sincere efforts to let go of distraction would have never happened (or lasted).

The pages that follow include three stories from my journey, which I hope will enable you to gain valuable awareness about the cost of your distraction. Then a "Hands Free Weekly Intention" offers a list of practical ways to help you curb your distracted tendencies and initiate meaningful interactions with the people you love. These intentions correspond with the letting-go action illustrated in the story. The intentions in this first chapter encourage you to take an honest look inward to assess the cost of your distractions.

Despite the pain you may experience while reading this chapter, do not let it discourage you. On this journey to grasp what really matters, discomfort often comes before growth; hurt before healing; regret before promise. By going to the darkest places in our soul, we find light. This first and most difficult step in the journey offers the chance of a new beginning—a chance to grasp the moments that matter from this day forward.

WHAT I WOULD HAVE MISSED

I still have the envelope. It's nestled among my most valuable documents, along with my marriage license, passport, social security card, and birth certificate—documents that prove I exist. It's not the content of the oversized envelope, stamped with the logo of our local zoo, that's worth saving—it's the message scribbled on the outside.

The words were written on the very day I vowed to stop missing the precious moments that make life worth living. Like rushing water from a swollen stream, the words filled my mind with such force that I was unable to hold them back. I scrambled through a kitchen drawer, looking for something to write on—as if my life depended on documenting these words.

At first glance, the uneven trail of words looks like a grocery list jotted while driving—imagine one hand holding the steering wheel while the other scribbles *eggs, milk,* and *broccoli.* There's no capitalization. The *t's* aren't crossed. The sentences have no punctuation. But all that only reveals my haste. I was certain I must remember every single word of this epiphany, which changed the course of my life. Here is a polished version of what I wrote:

> What if you missed hearing the best part of your child's day because you were on the phone?
>
> What if you missed a chance to inhale the sweet scent of your energetic child because you insisted on folding that basket of laundry before bedtime?
>
> What if you missed a chance to console your worried spouse because of your mile-long to-do list?
>
> What if you missed hearing an unknown childhood memory from your aging parent because you were too busy to call?
>
> What if you missed a divine cloud formation in the sky because you were racing to the bank, the post office, and the dry cleaner before you had to pick up the kids?
>
> What if one day you realized that all the opportunities you missed couldn't be retrieved?
>
> But it was already too late.
>
> What if one day you realized the best moments in life come in the mundane, everyday moments? But you were only fully present on special occasions.
>
> What if, instead of rushing through the minutiae of your daily life, you occasionally paused and offered your presence?
>
> What if you turned away from the distractions that monopolize your time and attention and grasped the sacred moments passing you by?
>
> Turn off the music in the car.
>
> Sit next to your child as she plays.
>
> Lie in bed with her after you say good night.
>
> Hug her and don't let go right away.
>
> Tell her something you have been meaning to say.
>
> Bend down and look her in the eye when she talks to you.

Do these things and see what might unfold. And once the moment is over, reflect back on that moment and realize this painful truth: If I had not paused, that precious moment is what I would have missed.

After covering the front and back of the envelope with my thoughts, I stared at it. Although not sure what I was supposed to do with what I'd written, I simply could not put the envelope back in the drawer. This once-ordinary envelope now exuded significance, so I set it on the counter with a sense of expectation—as if waiting for it to come to life.

I didn't have to wait long. Less than an hour later, the purpose of what I'd written became clear.

As I was making lunch as usual for my younger daughter, Avery, my laptop was open on the kitchen counter and my phone was an arm's length away. The devices battled for my attention with their respective dings and beeps. I answered their demanding summons with instant obedience.

Between incoming texts and email messages, I hurriedly applied peanut butter to a slice of bread. The sooner I could make my child's lunch, the sooner I could address a few pressing matters on my to-do list. My mind was preoccupied with an upcoming baby shower I was hosting, the low air pressure on the front right tire, and making copies of a community-picnic flier.

For some reason, I looked up. I knew my child was there, but this time I noticed her, really noticed her. My precious curly-haired daughter sat on the sofa sucking her thumb while gently rubbing her nose. Suddenly, I felt like I couldn't breathe. For the first time, I felt a new kind of urgency—an unsettling, uncomfortable, downright painful kind of urgency. *Time was running out.*

Then I did something atypical of my productive nature, something foreign to my type-A why-do-it-later-when-you-can-do-it-now mentality. Without even joining the two pieces of sandwich bread, I balanced the gooey knife on the open jar. Without closing the open bag of bread, without giving thought to the time, without contemplating the next item on the agenda, I went to my child. I felt God's presence encouraging me to let the other stuff go; nothing was more important than being with my daughter.

I sat down next to her and placed my arm around her small shoulders. She looked into my eyes, her whole face brightening.

Her wide eyes instantly transformed into joyful slices of happiness. Quickly filling the space between my body and hers, she scooted over and melted into me.

What happened next was something no one had ever done to me.

She brought my hand to her pink lips and ever so gently kissed my palm.

As my eyes filled with tears, I knew this was it. My confirmation. My divine sign. In one simple, beautiful gesture, my daughter cemented my newfound pursuit to live Hands Free. I realized with clarity that *this*—this pausing when the whole world keeps on going—is living.

I wanted more tender moments like this. But first I had to admit that they wouldn't be so rare if I would simply stop for a moment. The truth is: *No matter how much she wants to, needs to, or would love to, my child cannot kiss a moving target.*

Living distracted had cost me countless precious moments, but thank goodness I didn't miss this one—because it changed everything.

My moving-target days had officially come to an end.

 ## HANDS FREE WEEKLY INTENTION

Go Hands Free for a Specific Time Period Each Day

Living Hands Free does not mean giving up technology altogether, and it does not mean ignoring your job responsibilities, volunteer obligations, or home duties. Living Hands Free means making a conscious decision to temporarily push aside distractions and give your undivided attention to someone or something meaningful in your life.

I started my journey by designating time periods when I unplugged from my devices and connected to my loved ones. Because I was so dependent on technology, I had to start with short, ten-minute increments.

Although that doesn't seem like much, the results were profound. Here are some of the revelations I experienced during my initial Hands Free periods:

- A feeling of peace and contentment came over me when I was fully engaged with a loved one. I felt assured that I was exactly where I needed to be at that moment.
- Within minutes of spending time in meaningful connection, online activities and household duties suddenly lost their urgency. Emails, phone calls, dirty laundry, and scrolling newsfeeds would still be there after I finished nurturing my relationships—but time with my loved ones was fleeting.
- Opportunities to connect to loved ones became more apparent. My Hands Free inner voice began to grab me and gently encourage me by saying, "Come on, put the phone down. Turn off the computer. You're missing your life!" I realized that even in the midst of a busy day, there are countless opportunities to pause and connect with the people who matter most. I had just been too distracted to notice.
- Being constantly available to people outside my family and trying to stay current on all the latest online happenings was sabotaging my ability to live and love. The only person who could protect my time was me. And to do so, I had to create boundaries between technology and life.

As a result of these positive effects, I was motivated to increase the duration of my distraction-free time increments. With each experience of loving connection, my ties to daily distraction weakened.

This week, incorporate a designated Hands Free Time Period into your daily routine. Turn off your electronics—phone, tablet, laptop, or whatever—and then put them in a drawer or lock them in your car if you have to. Do whatever it takes to disconnect from devices and initiate meaningful connection with a loved one at least once a day. Here are a few examples of distraction-free time frames:

- first thing in the morning
- right before naptime or bedtime
- when children arrive home from school
- mealtimes
- from dinner time until bedtime

As you make room for these Hands Free Time Periods, pay attention to the positive results. What emotions do you experience when you step away from your devices to spend time with a loved one? Do you notice anything special about your loved one that you failed to notice before? Does the importance of your online activities decrease when you are engaged in a moment of loving human connection? Are you beginning to notice more opportunities to connect to what matters to you?

By shutting down your devices periodically each day, you are able to protect your time, strengthen your relationships, and nurture your own health and well-being. Giving yourself a chance to notice the details that make life worth living is time well spent.

CATCHING RAINBOWS

My daughters and I had just left the house for swim practice. We were less than five minutes from home when we noticed unusually dark clouds forming in the direction of the pool. As we discussed whether we should turn back, we heard the unmistakable sound of thunder.

Delighted by their unexpected day off from practice, the girls began to celebrate the impending rain with fits of laughter. As I turned the car around, my older daughter, Natalie, interrupted the impromptu party long enough to ask whether a celebration was truly in order.

"Do we have to *do* anything when we get home?" she cautiously asked the drill sergeant behind the steering wheel, who was known for having every spare moment accounted for and planned out.

The answer "Nope, not a thing" evoked cheers.

But when the garage door lifted, the open agenda I had just promised quickly filled. Somehow in our hasty comings and goings, I had failed to notice the disturbing state of our garage. The floor was littered with pool toys, winter gear, holiday decorations, and empty soda cans. It was a seasonal dumping ground. As I grabbed the industrial-size broom, I felt pleased to have this unexpected opportunity to get the garage back in order.

Donned in Hawaiian leis and ski masks, the girls began picking up random items so I could sweep the floor. As I glanced up to assess our trash-bag supply, a hushed, steady rain began to creep over our house. Despite the gentle precipitation, the sun was still shining in all its glory — a highly unusual weather phenomenon. I hesitated for a moment, wondering if I should mention it to the girls, who were being oddly productive. Not long ago, I would have kept quiet to avoid disturbing their efficiency.

But things were different now.

My Hands Free inner voice gently reminded me that I had never danced in the rain with my daughters.

I abruptly tossed the broom to the floor and ran to where the girls were crushing empty soda cans with enthusiasm. In a voice so urgent it actually startled them, I hollered, "Let's go see if there's a rainbow!" I darted out to our driveway, which was already dotted with tiny raindrops.

The girls quickly followed with delighted yet reserved smiles. Natalie looked like she was waiting for me to spoil the fun by adding, "But only for a minute. We don't want to get our clothes wet; plus we have lots of work to do!"

But when I extended my arms and began swirling in circles, my daughter relaxed and did the same with a look of pure joy on her face. For several moments, my children and I just stood there savoring the soft, slow rain as it tickled our bare arms.

Without warning, the silence of our enchanted moment was broken by urgent young voices from off in the distance. "Rainbow! Rainbow!" shouted two neighbor boys as they pointed excitedly to the west.

In our rain-induced reverie, my children and I had forgotten our initial intention. When we turned to look, our eyes filled with the most glorious sight. Not one, but two full-fledged rainbows! Miraculously, we could see their arches from end to end.

My daughters looked at me and then at each other with the most amazed expressions. "Thank you! Thank you!" I cried out with joy. The boys across the street probably thought I was thanking them, but my gratitude for that glorious moment was meant for God alone.

My children instinctively stretched their hands toward the sky. At first, I thought they wanted to feel the rain once more, knowing it soon would be gone. Then it appeared as if they were trying to grasp those colorful silk ribbons suspended in the vibrant sky. Finally, I decided it really didn't matter what the children were doing or why. For in that magical moment, we caught a double rainbow. And it would be ours forever.

 ## HANDS FREE WEEKLY INTENTION

Make a Priceless Investment

A critical step in my Hands Free journey was reevaluating what I considered a valuable use of my time. My highly distracted life was all about productivity. If I couldn't check off an activity on my to-do list, it held no value. But when I started viewing time spent with family or doing something I enjoyed as a Priceless Investment, I was able to make those moments a priority in my schedule. Leisurely activities I once viewed as time wasters were now esteemed as valuable contributions to my children's memory banks, my marriage, and my personal happiness.

One exercise that enabled me to dedicate more time and energy toward family connection was to define what daily distraction looked like. From this description, I could easily identify what factors prevented me from investing in the people I love. I used the following definition to become more aware of my distractions and avoid losing precious time to them.

Rachel's Definition of Daily Distraction includes anything that

- takes the focus off what truly matters
- prevents me from being fully present
- stops me from investing time and energy in people I love
- hinders my ability to slow down, relax, or get adequate sleep
- holds me back from enjoying life, taking risks, and being my authentic self

Other sabotaging factors include, but are not limited to

- phone (email and text messages)
- laptop computer (social media, blogs)
- television
- e-reader
- to-do lists
- overcommitment
- excessive feelings of worry, guilt, inadequacy, perfection, or self-doubt
- pressure to act or look a certain way

This week, make an investment of time, attention, and love in your treasured relationships by temporarily ditching distraction and being fully present. Start by identifying the sabotaging factors that prevent you from investing in what really matters. Ask yourself: What daily distractions prevent me from being fully present with the people I love? What actions can I take to reduce or eliminate one or more of these distractions?

By identifying your distractions, you can become more aware of their potential to weaken your relationships. This heightened awareness will enable you to make different choices. It is helpful to note that making valuable investments in the lives of your loved ones does not require enormous amounts of time and effort. For example, here are some highly achievable investments made by members of *The Hands Free Revolution* community:

- I left my phone in the car and walked hand in hand into school with my child.
- I conversed with my child in the car on the way to practice.
- I put my phone in the closet after work and played a game with my family.
- I read two extra books at bedtime.
- I made a snowman with my child.
- I let my child help make the salad.

Initially, it seemed like a daunting task to break my patterns of distracted behavior, but by breaking it down to one Hands Free increment at a time, it became possible. Every time I let go of a distraction, my choice was reinforced by my family's positive response to my presence. Never once did I regret letting go of distraction to make an investment in their lives. In fact, I found that by taking time to connect, I was rejuvenated and able to complete my work and home duties more effectively. And that, my friend, is what I call "gold" at the end of a Hands Free rainbow.

SUNSET MOMENTS

Shortly after my husband and I were married, we relocated from Indiana to Florida. The first year in our new surroundings was challenging. I was extremely homesick for my family and friends back home.

One evening I was driving home from work a little later than usual. I was heading west, and the horizon was in full view. I can still remember the comforting familiarity of John Mellencamp's raspy voice on the radio and the taste of tears on my lips. There was an empty feeling in the pit of my stomach, which I attributed to the longing I felt to see my parents.

Suddenly, as if someone had abruptly opened the curtains in a dark room, I was overwhelmed by a breathtaking display in front of me.

What was previously a typical evening sky was now a brilliant spectacle of pink, yellow, orange, and red. My eyes were drawn to the focal point of this unfolding masterpiece — the fiery wedge of the setting sun slipping over the horizon until it was completely gone, leaving in its wake wide brushstrokes of warmth and peace.

In that moment, my sadness slipped away as well. I felt an encouragement I hadn't known in months. The fact that I was in precisely the right location at exactly the right time to witness this display of hope was a great comfort to my broken soul.

Over the years, I've often thought about that particular sunset and how easily I could have missed it. There was a time not too long ago when I might have been talking on the phone, mentally reviewing a to-do list, or worse, quickly glancing at an incoming email or text message. By the grace of God, I was fully present and able to witness a once-in-a-lifetime Sunset Moment. Because, truth be told, this extraordinary sight would have happened whether or not I'd taken the time to watch. That astonishing display could have happened right in front of my face, but, had I been distracted, I would have missed it.

Now that I'm on a journey to grasp what really matters, I've discovered that everyday life has Sunset Moments too.

As my older daughter instinctively grasps my hand in the grocery-store parking lot and holds on far longer than necessary, I realize: This is a Sunset Moment.

As my husband and I sit with the television off and talk about everything from the antics of our children to how far we've come together, I realize: This is a Sunset Moment.

As I experience the tenacious strength of my sturdy legs that can run for miles without complaint, I realize: This is a Sunset Moment.

As I watch my seventy-four-year-old father make homemade ice cream with his doting granddaughters on the sunlit porch, I realize: This is a Sunset Moment.

Life's Sunset Moments are glorious, rejuvenating, and gratifying to behold—but when I'm caught up in daily distractions, they are so carelessly missed. If I just pretend to watch, I will miss them. If my hands are too busy doing other things, I will miss them. If my body is present, but my mind is not, I will miss them. If I hold on to distraction tighter than I grasp what really matters, I will miss Sunset Moments time and time again.

My highly distracted years cost me many precious moments. I can't get them back, and so I choose to focus on celebrating the possibilities that await me each new day. Just as the sun sets and rises again, each day offers a chance to grasp what truly matters despite the mistakes of the past. Although I may stumble along this journey toward a more meaningful life, experiencing a Sunset Moment is all I need to set my feet back on the right path. Because no matter what direction I'm heading, the Sunset Moments steer me toward the life I want to live.

 ## HANDS FREE WEEKLY INTENTION

Let Go of the To-Do List!

Early on in my Hands Free journey, I discovered my to-do list, like the phone and computer, was another daily distraction. As a letting-go strategy, I did something I never thought I was capable of doing. I took a match and burned my to-do list. The act itself was quite liberating, but the results were life changing. For a whole day, I did only what I felt most compelled to do—which was to write stories and connect with my family. A day later, I rewrote a much shorter to-do list because I could only remember the most pressing things. I let go of the items I couldn't remember. Miraculously, the world did not end, and I realized I had to stop allowing my to-do list to dictate my life.

Don't get me wrong, I still use a calendar to keep track of appointments and commitments. But my to-do list is no longer as central as it once was. I can go for days without looking at it now that I've created a powerful Life List (which we'll talk about in chapter 7). In addition, I use one-item reminder notes rather than exhaustive lists to remember important tasks. The quick-and-easy sticky note allows me to be dependable yet Hands Free because I am not bogged down by an overwhelming list of duties.

This week, set aside your to-do list for a time period of your choosing and embrace the freedom to engage in the callings of your heart. At first it might seem scary and you might feel lost. But do it anyway. Give yourself a chance to experience the meaningful connections you seldom have time for when strapped to a list. When you eventually make your way back to your list, you may find an enlightened perspective on which tasks truly need to be accomplished and which can be eliminated completely.

By stepping away from your to-do list, the Sunset Moments of your life have a chance to come into full view. One blog reader shared her experience of letting go of the pressure to be productive in favor of relishing time with her child: "I felt like I had super senses. I felt the slight, rhythmic rise and fall of her chest. I felt the silky smoothness of her little hands. I smelled the singular scent of her skin and watched the wonder in her eyes. I honestly felt reborn. It truly was a Sunset Moment for me and I can't wait to make more. They are rejuvenating and worth every second of what I would previously had called wasted time."

We all have tasks, but we must not let them prevent us from seeing once-in-a-lifetime opportunities to grasp what really matters. Rather than viewing your to-do list as something you cannot function without, consider it a tool for managing a fulfilling Hands Free life.

 HANDS FREE REFLECTION

Awareness Reminders

Every now and then, I experience Hands Free reminders—moments when my child suddenly looks grown up or says something profound … moments when time slaps me in the face and says, "Pay attention. This won't last forever."

Every now and then, I need to be reminded that having to sweep up the crumbs beneath her chair is not really a problem.

I need to be reminded that the times when she grasps my hand as we cross a busy street or asks me to "C'mere and see this ladybug" are moments to stop and savor.

I need to be reminded that I could complain less, cherish more, let go of the have-tos, and say yes more often.

I need to be reminded that although sunsets and goodbyes happen every day, each one should be treated as if it's the last.

I need to be reminded that real living happens when I peel away the distractions and hold my perfectly imperfect life tenderly in my hands.

Because that day will come sooner than I think, when I stand inside her bedroom closet and I'll be able to see the floor. There will be no brightly colored clothes haphazardly hung from hangers along the narrow walls, no dirty clothes that missed the mark of the hamper.

And I will place my hand on all that is left. And when I do, I will be so grateful that I hugged her that day rather than scolding her for writing her name on the wall of the closet.

Because in the end, a moment of exasperation will be just as much a gift as a moment of joy—only without the pretty packaging.

So I intend to keep grasping the reminders.

And someday, I'll be grateful I didn't miss my life.

REFLECTION QUESTIONS

What do you consider a valuable use of your time? Does your daily agenda reflect this?

Have your distractions taken an undeserved position on your priority list?

What parts of life do you not want to miss?

What are you going to do to ensure that you are grasping the moments that matter today so you don't live with regret tomorrow?

Chapter 2

MAKE PURPOSEFUL CONNECTION

Connectedness

The most precious gift we can offer others is our presence. When mindfulness embraces those we love, they will bloom like flowers.

Thich Nhat Hanh

THE KISS ON MY PALM left a powerful imprint. In one intimate gesture, my daughter showed me what she needed, what I needed, and what we both had been desperately missing: meaningful connection. That kiss empowered me to do something I thought was impossible: seize opportunities to connect—regardless of my agenda. That kiss inspired me to dance with my daughters when the garage needed cleaning. That kiss inspired me to assist my child with a puzzle when my email inbox was frighteningly full. That kiss inspired me to join my family on the porch to marvel at the moon when dirty dishes cluttered the sink. That kiss on my palm was far more rewarding than any to-do accomplishment, and it only required a small investment of time. That is when the next step of my journey revealed itself. Making purposeful connection with someone or something meaningful was vital to transforming my distracted life. And this step alone proved to be life changing.

Whether I chose to go Hands Free for ten minutes or two hours, a profoundly transforming reaction occurred every single time. With each effort to be fully present with a loved one, I experienced a sense of peace, fulfillment, and gratitude that was foreign to my hurried and distracted existence. Suddenly, I found a way to make time stand still. Meaningless tasks I once deemed important were quickly demoted on the priority list. Nothing was more important than being with the God-given gift of the person in front of me. I yearned to experience this powerful reaction again and again until it became routine.

The three stories that follow are about making a meaningful connection with the people who matter. The Hands Free Weekly Intentions offer strategies to help you let go of distraction and engage with others. When you take time each day to grasp what really matters, distractions of the digital age cannot sabotage your relationships, your dreams, your memories, or your pursuit of a present and joy-filled life.

MY SECRET LIFE

When I first decided to live Hands Free, I didn't tell a soul—not my spouse, parents, children, or closest friends. For three months, I kept my small daily efforts a secret.

Although the feelings of connection to my family were immediate and profound, I still revealed nothing about what I was trying to do.

Kind of like a New Year's resolution ... in my head.

Or announcing a new life goal ... to myself.

Because it felt scary to put myself out there. After all, I might fail, or someone might hold me accountable.

Fear of failure and accountability were precisely why I kept my Hands Free endeavor to myself. I had been holding so tightly to distraction that it had become a way of life. My constant checking of my electronic devices and my jam-packed schedule enabled me to avoid facing difficult truths.

What if I couldn't stop living my highly distracted life?

What if it was easier to ignore that little voice that kept urging me there was a better way to live?

But that's not what happened.

Within days of beginning to live Hands Free, I felt like I'd stepped into a new life. As my hands were freed, my eyes were opened. And what I saw were hundreds of opportunities to connect with what really mattered. I had been too distracted, too hurried, too stressed out to see them before.

For the first time in a long time, I had the ability to stop and catch my breath.

For the first time in a long time, I was not just managing life, I was living it.

There was no contest: looking into my children's eyes beat staring at the screen of my smartphone. Hearing my loved ones' laughter won hands down over the incessant ding of incoming emails. Seeing empty space in my calendar for laughing, playing, and relaxing soothed my depleted soul.

I was sold on living Hands Free, and I was ready to tell someone.

I started with my husband, Scott. And because I prefer writing down my thoughts to speaking them, I typed my intentions and shared with him how our daughter had kissed my palm.

Scott didn't say much at first. I could tell he was processing the idea. But the next day when he returned from an outing with our kids, I could tell he had something important to tell me.

Once we were alone, he said he couldn't stop thinking about the concept of being Hands Free. While at the children's museum that morning, he'd noticed several parents who paid more attention to their phones than to their kids. This observation motivated him to turn off his phone, push away thoughts of work, and focus solely on our children's clever comments and beautiful expressions. In doing so, he felt a strong sense of connection, peace, and renewal.

That was the moment I knew I needed to go public with my Hands Free journey. Within three months, I published my first blog post.

But here's the sad thing: while I told the world I was going Hands Free, I didn't tell my children.

What?

Granted, my children knew about the Hands Free Mama blog; they were familiar with the term *Hands Free* and even used the phrase when someone (mostly our movie-loving second child) carried a portable DVD player to the dinner table. We often talked about the importance of not using the phone while driving, but never did I say, "I am striving to live Hands Free, and *you* are the reason. *You*, my precious children who are growing before my very eyes, are the reason I don't want to miss any Sunset Moments."

So why didn't I tell them?

Because I couldn't bear for those two particular people to see my flaws, shortcomings, weaknesses—to see that I am far from perfect and have a lot of work to do.

But soon I knew I needed to tell them. It was time.

So I chose two beautiful journals in which my children could write down anything they wanted to talk about with me. But as I wrote my entry message on the first page, my Hands Free inner voice urged me to go further. I found myself writing, "If there is anything I need to work on to be a better parent, please write it in here. I want to live Hands Free to grasp what really matters—and *you* are what really matters."

Requesting constructive criticism does not come easily for a recovering perfectionist like myself. But if there is anything I have learned on this Hands Free journey, it is this: *The truth hurts, but the truth heals—and brings me closer to the person I aspire to be.*

I wasn't expecting my children to be overly excited about their journals. In fact, I didn't think Avery, my younger daughter, would "get it." But if there is another thing I've learned on this journey, it is that the most meaningful things often come unexpectedly and unplanned. The most life-changing experiences happen when I stop trying to control and simply let things unfold.

I was not expecting what was to come.

Avery has asked to write in her journal every night since she received it. And although I only described the purpose of the journal to her once, she nailed it by going straight to my heart within its pages.

When I most needed it, Avery provided food for my hungry soul: "You are the most beautiful mom," she wrote in bright blue gel pen with hearts all around the words.

Soon after that, when I was becoming overly consumed with my writing, Avery gave me a dose of reality: "Each person in our family has a problem they need to work on. Yours is that you write too many stories," my daughter informed me while drawing a picture of me with my open laptop.

When she needed something, Avery told me exactly what she desired to feel loved and valued: "I like to have alone time with you," she wrote in large, bold letters.

And when feelings of guilt overwhelm me, I find this recurring message in my child's journal: "I love you" is written on almost every page. She knows those words can never be said or heard too much.

Through her entries, she reminds me that living Hands Free is not about being perfect; nor is it about being hyperfocused on the people I love. It is simply about making a conscious effort each and every day to connect.

Through Avery's drawings and words, I can see what a Hands Free life looks like:

It is togetherness.

It is communication.

It is forgiveness.

It is unconditional love.

Each time I take a moment to read and reread these direct reflections of my child's heart, I am overwhelmed with undeniable proof—proof that I cannot create a Hands Free life while holding tightly to distraction. I am determined now, more than ever, to continue filling the pages of my own beautifully flawed yet memorable and gratitude-filled life.

Today you too are presented with a blank page. A beautifully flawed, memorable, and gratitude-filled life is at your fingertips.

All you have to do is open your hands.

And say yes.

Say it loud enough for the world to hear.

Or just say it loud enough for the people who matter most to hear.

 ## HANDS FREE WEEKLY INTENTION

Go Public

I remember exactly where I was and what I said when I revealed my Hands Free aspirations to the important people in my life. Although it was difficult to find the words, I felt a sense of freedom when I made my intentions known. I was concerned that my declaration might cause some loved ones to look over my shoulder and chide me every time I committed a "distraction infraction." But that was not the case. Their involvement in my journey motivated me to stay the course and be fully present in designated Hands Free Time Periods. Rather than feeling like I was under a microscope, I felt an additional source of support fueling my journey.

An unexpected result of Going Public was the positive feedback I received. My mom said, "Your dad and I can't believe the difference in you, Rachel! You're happier now ... more patient and relaxed. This Hands Free journey is changing you!" I'm grateful both of my parents are alive to see I have changed and no longer worry that I will die an early death due to overcommitment, excessive stress, and texting at stoplights.

Sharing my intentions with my family and friends was difficult, but the outcome was so positive that I wish I'd done it sooner.

Make a Hands Free declaration by telling the important people in your life what Hands Free means to you. Explain why you feel it's important to curb your technology use and how they can help you be successful. Choose one of the following intentions or create one of your own:

- "I may need help remembering to put my phone away when I drive (eat dinner, go on family outings). Could you have a conversation with me instead?"
- "I may need encouragement to remain unplugged when you get home from school because I would really like to stay off my computer until you go to bed."
- "I would like to have one media-free evening each week. Would you join me?"
- "I'm going to attempt to have one day (or night) a week when I don't use any electronic devices. Would you like to do this together?"

Not only will going public with your Hands Free aspirations help you stay the course, but you may also inspire someone else to curb their device usage. Instead of being a Hands Free individual, you might find you've become part of a Hands Free couple or Hands Free family, like this inspiring reader:

A few weeks ago we had dinner with some family friends. Their child was complaining of being bullied at school and on Facebook. The entire time he had his head down in his phone. He missed the conversation, the laughs, and the ability to connect with the adults and his friends at the table.

When we left the restaurant my son hugged me and said, "Mom, I am so happy we are a Hands Free family."

He and I both had tears in our eyes. It is moments like these that will change your life and help your child grow. Be the inspiration they need to turn off the tech and turn up the real life relationships they so desperately need.

START THE CONVERSATION

My family and I were dining at a new local restaurant. With packed tables and an attentive waitstaff, it had a bustling but jovial atmosphere. Sitting next to us was a couple about the same age as my husband and me. They sat closely, side by side, so I assumed they were dating or perhaps married.

But there was one problem: they weren't talking.

The man had a firm grip on his phone, which was perched directly under his nose. He looked like a dog guarding a bone. His companion, completely empty-handed, stared blankly ahead, and she looked more than sad—she looked empty.

I tried not to stare. Their detachment was none of my business, and besides, my preoccupation with them was causing me to be anything but Hands Free with my own family. Yet something compelled me to keep watching them.

For the next twenty minutes, the woman never attempted to engage her distracted companion in conversation. She stared straight ahead, except for one brief moment when she glanced over at our table. When my younger daughter sang a made-up tune and used her chopsticks as props, the alienated woman smiled brightly. She looked like a completely different person than she had moments before. Sadly, the woman's smile quickly faded as if she'd been struck by a brutal reality: she was admiring someone else's life.

"Hey, Hands Free Mama," Scott whispered to me, "stop staring. You're as distracted as he is."

I knew he was right. Who was I to judge? I kept hoping the dining disaster would turn itself around. I wished that the distracted man would abruptly put the phone away, apologize to his companion (perhaps update her on a terminally ill relative), and then tenderly reach for her hand.

But he didn't.

He put the phone down briefly when the waitress brought his food, but within seconds, he resumed his focus on the small electronic screen as he brought his fork to his mouth.

I'm not one for confrontation, but I ached to walk over and gently point out the opportunity he was missing. "Don't you see that beautiful woman sitting next to you? Can't you see she wants you to notice her and talk to her? Is whatever you're doing on the phone *really* more important than the human being at your table?"

Of course, I didn't have the nerve, but I couldn't let it go either. As we drove home that night, I was still fuming. Why was I so angry with the man with the phone? Why such a protest about his behavior? The answers were not easy—because grasping what really matters means going to the tender places in one's soul. And when I took an honest look, I admitted that out of all the areas in my life that I had rescued from the damage of distraction, I had failed to protect one area as fiercely as the others.

My relationship with my husband.

There. I said it. And with that difficult truth came life-changing awareness. I decided to do something about my problem. Because taking even a small step in the Hands Free journey gets me that much closer to grasping what really matters in this one precious life.

In the months following the scene at the restaurant, I made small but impactful changes to protect my romantic relationship from drowning in distractions:

- I went to lunch with my husband for the first time in eight years. I'd had enough of the excuses "I'm too busy" or "his office is too far away." We even made plans for the next lunch date—and it wasn't eight years away.
- I watched the entire Super Bowl planted right by his side—something I'd never done in our fifteen years of marriage.
- I converted a plain notebook into an "Appreciation Journal" for my husband. In it, I wrote him short thank-you notes that ranged from appreciating little things (an unexpected full tank of gas, joining me for a jog) to the big things (being such a present and loving father and husband).

- I started asking more questions about his workday. More importantly, I started really listening to his responses.
- I occasionally presented him with cards—not for any particular reason, just to say, "I love you."
- I became more mindful about giving him a proper hug and kiss before we went our separate ways each day.
- On the weekend, I put away my writing projects so we had ample time for meaningful connection.

The last one was the hardest. My writer's brain has a difficult time shutting off.

But when I do let go of my distraction, I look back and wonder why it was so hard to stop writing and just *be* with the one I love.

Like on one particular Saturday night ...

Earlier that day, our daughters asked where my husband and I went on our first date. Naturally, the topic was still on our minds a few hours later when we had a chance to be alone. Scott and I began reminiscing about that fateful night. Soon we were not only laughing about that stubborn wad of gum that got stuck to the backside of my jeans, but also how his college roommate sat us down and demanded we tell each other how we really felt about each other.

In the midst of our discussion, I admitted how I fell head over heels the night he changed my flat tire.

He didn't know.

And he described the way he felt when he handed me the first real Valentine he'd ever given someone.

I didn't know.

By the end of our conversation, we were both experiencing that spark we felt when we first fell in love. Compound that feeling with fifteen years of marriage, and we felt closer than ever. With painful awareness, I realized that this particular conversation would not have happened if I had chosen instead to spend that evening writing.

Although I didn't have a phone glued to my face, I realized I need to continually evaluate whether my wi-fi connection is taking precedence over my marriage connection. Because I'm in it for the long haul, which means investing time, focus, energy, and love into the man I'm crazy about. And with my eyes focused on what really matters, I see a beautiful future.

 **HANDS FREE WEEKLY INTENTION**

Start the Conversation

Protecting my marriage from the damage of distraction was a challenging step in my Hands Free journey. And it's an area of weakness I must constantly evaluate. Zoning out in front of a screen after the children go to bed is a strong temptation. The urge to pull out the phone during waiting situations, even when I'm with my spouse, is intense. There is a mentality in today's society regarding electronic devices and romantic relationships that I once believed too:

> *So what if we sit side by side on the couch every night using our individual handheld devices and laptops? So what if we check our smartphones at the dinner table, in the car, and while on a date? What's the big deal? We have the rest of our lives to spend time together.*

It wasn't until I honestly assessed how often I reached for my phone in the presence of my spouse that my behavior changed. Much like going Hands Free with my children, I started by designating small increments of time to be distraction-free with my spouse. These intentional periods grew from minutes to hours, from days to weeklong vacations. Engaging in regular, purposeful connection has made a significant impact on our relationship. We are closer than we've been in fifteen years of marriage. We go for entire weekends without looking at our phones. But most of all, we look forward to those times of peaceful connection so we can be reminded of why we fell in love in the first place.

This week, schedule daily or weekly undistracted, uninterrupted time with the love of your life.

Chances are, you will experience a heightened awareness about your tendency to reach for the phone. Try to avoid justifying your behavior with excuses like "well, she always gets her phone out" or "he constantly checks his device, so I may as well check mine." Instead of making excuses, remember:

Someone has to start a new way of waiting at the restaurant . . .

Someone has to start a new way of waiting at your child's sporting event . . .

Someone has to start a new way of waiting for the concert to begin . . .

Someone has to Start the Conversation.

Let it be you.

Because every time you engage in conversation with the person you love, you give your relationship a fighting chance.

HOW'S MY DRIVING?

As I drove my usual carload of children down our neighborhood streets, I saw brake lights ahead flashing erratically. Accompanying the jerky stops, the car ahead swerved side-to-side. I worried that the driver might be intoxicated, but as I got closer, the reason became obvious. In fact, the reason was perched right next to the steering wheel for the whole world to see. With phone in hand, the driver was attempting to type a text message while driving his children to school.

I nervously glanced at the happy kids walking to school along the sidewalk. I prayed no child would lose his or her footing or playfully jump into the street.

After the fifth swerve and another sudden flash of brake lights, I could contain my anger no longer. "Put down your phone!" I screamed as if the man could hear me through my closed windows. Immediately, all four children in the back of my car craned their necks to see what was going on. They quickly spotted the driver focused on his phone.

Natalie made this astute observation: "Look at the kids in the backseat. That man could be talking to them instead of typing on his phone."

Just as I opened my mouth to agree with her insightful remark, Avery added her two cents—and what she said felt like a punch in the gut: "That man should be talking to his kids like Miss Mary talks to us when she drives us to school."

Suddenly my distraction radar swung from the erratic driver to the one behind my steering wheel. Why hadn't my daughter said, "He should be talking to his kids like *you* do, Mom."

I knew there was a reason, and I needed to do some painful soul searching to figure it out.

The truth hurts, but the truth heals.

Although I only use the phone in the car on rare occasions and have stopped the dangerous practice of checking email and text messages at stoplights, I hadn't taken the Hands Free concept to its fullest potential. Refraining from phone use while driving is only half the "letting go" equation. As I thought back, I realized I have a tendency to zone out behind the wheel. Driving had become a quiet time of collecting my thoughts and taking a breather. While there's nothing wrong with that practice in itself, I could have picked a better time to do it. With acute awareness, I thought about the conversations I had missed, the details of their school day that I didn't hear, the burdens resting on my children's hearts that I would never know.

Although it is tragic to drive with a phone in front of one's face, failing to connect with loved ones is tragic too. But before I went too far down the unproductive road of regret, my Hands Free inner voice reminded me that those mistakes were in the past. The hopeful part of living Hands Free is not about the past; it is about the critical choices we make today. Therefore, I used my child's comment as motivation to begin a new way of driving.

Here are a few of the small but powerful Hands Free efforts

that have allowed me to make meaningful connections while transporting my children:

Storytelling. All kids love a good story. So a few days a week, I tell my passengers a two-minute story, usually involving getting lost in Candy Land or a silly character I created when my girls were small. I love to watch their delighted eyes and wide smiles as they soak up the comical stories while we drive.

Hypothetical Questions. I go beyond the usual questions and ask questions like these:

- If you were an adult and didn't have to go to school today, how would you spend your day?
- If you had one hundred dollars, what would you do with it?
- If you could live anywhere, where would you live and why?
- What was the best dream you ever had?
- If you had three wishes, what would you wish for?
- If you saw a homeless person and could give him or her anything, what would you give?

I'm amazed at how these kinds of questions bring out interesting bits of information and create discussion.

Share a Memory. My children love to hear what life was like when I was in elementary school. I share stories of being bullied and what I would do differently now. I describe how I walked to my dad's office every day after school, toting my black violin case. I tell about my worst school pictures and my favorite teachers. Sharing my childhood memories creates laughter and brings out details of the children's school day that are sometimes difficult to extract.

Get into the Music. One of my children's favorite car activities is what we call a "seated dance party," which is basically playing loud music and bouncing around in our seats (with our seatbelts on). Whether it's that overly played vacation Bible school CD or the latest teen pop sensation, I grant their request to crank up the volume. That day will come (probably sooner than I think) when I am longing to hear those joyful voices coming from the backseat of the car.

A few weeks after making an effort to connect to my passengers, my commitment was sealed. When I informed the carpool children that it was not my turn to pick them up that day, one of the children whispered to the others, "I love it when Ms. Rachel picks us up. She's fun and makes me laugh." From that moment on, Rachel the Zoned-Out Driver was permanently replaced by Rachel the Interactive Driver.

I am simply the messenger on this Hands Free journey, and it is by the grace of God and four little carpool girls that I have this message to give. If zoning out, being on autopilot, or popping in a DVD have become part of your drive-time ritual—consider the tragedy:

- conversations that will never happen
- concerns on your child's heart and mind you will never hear
- smiles in the rearview mirror you will never see

You may not be holding your phone next to the steering wheel as you drive, but you just might be distracted in other ways.

Think about it.

Not many tragedies are preventable—but this one is.

 ## HANDS FREE WEEKLY INTENTION

Turn Drive Time into Connection Time

Turning off the notifications on my phone and placing it out of reach while driving was the easiest, yet most impactful effort in my Hands Free journey. With one simple action, I removed the temptation to check my phone. No longer summoned by the incessant dings, I was able to be fully present. Immediately, the entire atmosphere of the vehicle changed. In response to my attentiveness, my children began providing details about their school day and sharing their worries, dreams, and interests. Within days, drive time with my loved ones became such a valuable gift that every distracting phone conversation was worth sacrificing.

Although being Hands Free behind the wheel is vital to opening lines of communication, there is an even more critical reason to become an undistracted driver. Several months into my journey, I realized that my current driving habits predicted my children's future driving habits. Modeling Hands Free driving to my children now may likely result in my future teenagers following Hands Free driving practices later. It was painful for me to acknowledge that all those times I read email messages at stoplights or held the phone to my ear while driving, my children were watching and learning. But things are different now. Anytime I am tempted, I simply ask myself: "Would you want your daughters to do this right now?" The answer inspires me to put distraction in its proper place.

This week, take one step to remove the phone-use temptation while driving and use that time to engage in meaningful connection. Implement one of the following tactics:*

- Turn off phones or other devices before starting the car.
- Change your voice mail greeting to indicate you are driving and will call back when safely parked.
- Put your phone in your trunk or glove box.
- Put your phone in silent mode.
- If you need to contact someone, pull over to a safe location and park before dialing.
- Inform clients, associates, and business partners that calls will be returned when no longer driving.

Let today be a turning point in your life and in the lives of those you love. Let today be the day you put the phone away while driving.

---

*These are adapted from "On the Road Off the Phone," from the National Safety Council, last modified 2011, nsc.org/nsc_events/Nat_Safe_Month/Documents/OntheRoadOffthePhone.pdf.

HANDS FREE REFLECTION

Connectedness

The audience was totally captivated as her small, agile fingers played the last chords of "Rainbow Dreams" on the shiny piano keys. With quick strides, the golden-haired child made her way to her family sitting in the fifth row. After exchanging wide smiles with her grandpa, she placed her hand gently upon his arm. This was not accidental, nor was it a casual brush of the hand. This was a purposeful, loving connection. I am certain of this because the little girl did not remove her hand for quite some time. She rested it upon her grandfather's robust arm as they listened to other musicians.

I could not tear my eyes away. This tiny porcelain hand upon an elderly man's black tweed coat was the most beautiful sight my distracted eyes had ever seen.

In that one simple gesture,

I saw hope for the young.

I saw hope for the aging.

I saw hope for those in between.

I saw hope for today.

I saw hope for tomorrow.

I saw hope for the minutes in between.

I saw hope for the distracted.

I saw hope for the hurried.

I saw hope for you and for me.

In one simple gesture, a profound statement was made. There is no distraction in the world stronger than human connection. The distractions of the modern age cannot win our most valued possessions: our relationships, our memories, and our precious lives if we take a moment each day to put our hands on what matters most.

REFLECTION QUESTIONS

Is there a particular relationship that suffers more than others as a result of your distractions?

What might be the long-term impact on this relationship if you do not curb your distracted ways?

What anxieties or concerns do you have about letting go of your distractions? Could you share them with someone?

What are some of the positive results you've experienced when choosing connection over distraction?

Chapter 3

CHOOSE WHAT MATTERS

Deliberateness
~~∽⌒∽~~

At least three times every day take a moment and ask yourself what is really important. Have the wisdom and the courage to build your life around your answer.

Dr. Lee Jampolsky

YOU ARE FAR ENOUGH ALONG IN YOUR JOURNEY to understand an important notion about grasping what really matters. Living distracted causes you to miss priceless moments of connection that cannot be retrieved. Living Hands Free, on the other hand, allows you to experience the joy that comes from being fully engaged with others. Now that you are able to weigh the high costs of distraction against the priceless benefits of connection, the choice is yours. The next step is to recognize the positive impact that mindful daily choices can have on your relationships.

When I began my Hands Free journey, I expected that it would require one monumental and heroic action to overcome my distracted ways. But it turned out to be much simpler. I soon realized it was the small, everyday decisions about how I used my time and energy that kept me on a path to a more connected life.

Small amounts of time, energy, and attention became the building blocks of the meaningful life I wanted to live and the childhood I wanted my children to have. Knowing it was my decision to accept or reject these opportunities empowered me to seize the moments at hand. The other "stuff" would still be there when I finished reading to my child, conversing with my spouse, or looking into my child's eyes while she talked about her day. It soon became evident that consistently choosing connection over distraction was the key to a more joy-filled life—and to avoiding the pain and regret of missed opportunities.

Understanding that you have a choice is vitally important to a Hands Free life. Through the stories and weekly intentions contained in this chapter, I hope you will experience the personal fulfillment that comes from making intentional daily choices about how you spend your limited time and resources. Be prepared for an unexpected bonus: the choices you make to hold on to what matters will be noticed and appreciated by the people who matter—filling not only your heart with joy, but theirs as well.

I CHOOSE YOU

I wanted all household tasks to be completed as efficiently as possible. The control freak in my head believed if the job couldn't be accomplished perfectly by someone else, I had to do it myself. But that changed one memorable day when I stumbled out of the laundry room hoisting a mountainous basket of clean clothes. As I let the basket hit the floor with a thud, Avery asked if she could help me fold. For some odd reason, I agreed. My child didn't fold a lot of items that day, but she did a dance in her daddy's boxer shorts that had me laughing until I cried. It was when I wiped away those joyful tears that I finally saw the light.

Completing household responsibilities alone was cheating myself—and cheating my children. Doing household chores together was a not-so-obvious opportunity to grasp what really mattered. Yes, with a small child's help, the completion time and mess factor dramatically increased—but so did the laughter, joy, and memory making.

After that laundry-folding experience, Avery continued to offer her services. One night, she asked if she could wash the bowls and measuring cups we'd used to make muffins. I agreed, though only after a four-second delay. Before the words "Sure, you can help" came out of my mouth, my inner drill sergeant got in a few jabs. The thought of two inches of water on the floor made me cringe.

But those qualms were silenced the minute my daughter enthusiastically ran to get the stool she used to reach the sink. Back in a flash, she had the scrubber in hand and was practically drooling as I squeezed a stream of dishwashing soap into a bowl in the sink. As soon as the bowl filled with translucent bubbles, she put down the scrubber and eagerly reached for a handful of the magical suds.

At this point, I had a choice.

Here was my daughter happily playing in the bubbles, oblivious to everything going on around her. I could easily have started wiping down the counters and putting away the baking supplies. Or better yet, I could have sat down at the kitchen table and perused the glossy new magazine that beckoned me from the mail stack. But instead I chose what really mattered. I chose *who* really mattered.

I chose the little girl whose strawberry-blonde curls often resemble dreadlocks because of her strong aversion to hairbrushes. *I know full well that soon those knots will be replaced by soft, untangled strands of silk combed without my assistance.*

I chose the little girl who is still small enough to require a stool to wash her hands and rinse the family's dishes. *I know full well that someday she will be tall enough to reach the sink without a stool, and she will have better things to do than wash dishes with her mom.*

I chose the little girl who sings beautiful made-up songs about enormous bubbles carrying her up to heavenly blue skies. *I know someday she will be too mature to sing her self-created tunes, and it will be a rare treat to hear her lovely singing voice.*

55

With the kitchen in disarray and a million things to do, I chose my daughter. Because I still can. Today my child stands before me wanting, needing, and hoping to be chosen. Tomorrow might be different.

After a moment of watching my beautiful "choice" in all her glory, I scooped up a handful of bubbles and began stretching them into oblong shapes. My daughter smiled in amazement—amazed at the bubble formations or amazed that her mama was playing with them, I'm not sure which. She began imitating my movements with her own mound of bubbles.

As the bowl of soapy water sparkled in the dim kitchen light, I was suddenly transformed into a four-year-old version of myself. I could recall standing on a kitchen chair, holding the dish mop and smoothing all the soapy strings upward. To me, this was no dish mop. It was a beautiful doll who was receiving the most fabulous up-do hairstyle. My mom leaned in beside me and asked if it was time for the ball. (It wasn't a dish mop to her either.) My mom was smiling her beautiful smile, the one she still has today that makes me feel loved from the inside out.

I felt compelled to share this memory with my daughter. Simply saying "When I was a little girl" caused her to stop and look directly into my eyes. I told her about my princess dish mop. I told her all about the gorgeous soapy hairstyles. I told her about how my mom, her grandmother, would watch me and never once tell me to get back to washing the dishes. I told her how I played with my dish mop for so long that my fingers became wrinkly like prunes.

Avery looked entranced, absorbing every detail. The look on her face told me she loved this story and hungered for more details about her mother's childhood. I made a vow in that moment that I would be intentional about sharing more of my early life experiences with my daughters. After all, if I didn't take time to share my childhood memories with my children now, they might be lost forever.

"Look, Mama!" my daughter's enthusiastic voice interrupted my nostalgic reverie. She held up a bubble sculpture that resembled a glistening heart.

As I marveled at her unique creation and looked at her small hands encased in the magical bubbles, I recalled the poignant comment a reader made on my blog: "Being responsible for someone's childhood is a big deal. We not only create our own memories, but we create our child's memories."

If I simply allow this critical truth to guide my choices about how I spend my time, effort, energy, and focus, then I will be more apt to choose what really matters over the distractions of the digital age.

The memories my children carry with them into adulthood are largely up to me. In the everyday routines of life, I have the power to provide my children with countless loving memories of human connection. I also have the ability to leave my children with a scarce supply of meaningful moments together.

The choice is in my hands. For now, I want to continue to fill our days with bubbles, laughter, and love. And perhaps one day a powerful memory will bring us together beneath the dim light of a kitchen sink, even when we are miles and miles apart.

 ## HANDS FREE WEEKLY INTENTION

Engage in Household Tasks Together

Consider the mundane routines of your life. These are the moments that will someday become your grown children's memories. What would your children's memories of today be? Would it be how you paid more attention to your phone than you did to them? Would it be how you cleaned the entire house without managing to look them in the eyes? Would it be that every time they asked you to play you were "too busy"? Or would they remember how you laughed while washing the car together? How you let her crack the eggs at breakfast? How you tossed the ball to each other after dinner? Or how you patiently encouraged him while he struggled with math homework?

Letting go of my need for efficiency didn't happen overnight. Yet starting out with small jobs that we could do together was an instrumental step in my transformation. Even at age four, my daughter was able to help make salad for dinner, sweep the floors, and make beds. Okay, so folding the towels sometimes turned into a fashion show and washing the dishes sometimes turned into a science experiment, but we were spending time together — and that's what's important.

Not only does sharing in household tasks offer connection, but it helps children understand that these tasks don't magically get completed by themselves. As members of the family, they have an obligation to share in the responsibilities. Plus, there is no reason these tasks can't be enjoyable. While working together, we talk, share memories, dance, and act silly. Things don't have to be perfect. There are messes, but everyone helps clean up.

Invite your children to help you in one of your daily or weekly house-hold duties:

- dusting
- putting away toys
- preparing dinner
- setting the table
- cleaning windows
- walking or bathing the family pet
- folding laundry

While the tasks may not get accomplished quickly or perfectly, there is something far more critical at stake. Time spent together in mundane, everyday acts is the key to enhancing our most sacred relationships and filling our memory banks with love.

SOMEONE IS WAITING FOR YOU

Early in my journey, I was presented with the ultimate test to resist electronic distraction. Natalie had a medical concern that required several visits to a specialist. Because this particular doctor had a glowing reputation, the waiting room was always packed and patience was mandatory. Waiting to see the doctor meant sitting in a tiny room with no windows and no good magazines, surrounded by people staring at their phones.

If it weren't for my Hands Free commitment, I would have been right there with the rest of them. In fact, before I became Hands Free, I too passed time by using my phone. There were many doctor visits before this one when my daughters read books or played with blocks while I checked email messages, perused social media, or sent text messages.

But things are different now.

Wait Time had become Connection Time. After all, when you're waiting, there's nothing else you really *have* to do; there's nowhere else to go. So why not be—really be—with the loved one sitting next to you?

Here is how our two-hour wait at the doctor's office became more than bearable—it became a gift.

THE FIRST THIRTY-MINUTE PERIOD

During the first block of Wait Time, my children and I read through the letters Natalie had received from Priscilla, the Ghanaian child she sponsors through Compassion International. We read Priscilla's letters several times. In contrast to the quick way we typically read them at home, we actually had time to talk in detail about the content and pictures. I had time to answer every question that came to my daughter's mind. Then my daughter wrote a thoughtful letter back to Priscilla. And she lovingly decorated the edges of the paper with hearts, flowers, and smiley faces.

If I had chosen to spend that time looking at my phone, I would have missed this moment of connection and compassion.

THE SECOND THIRTY-MINUTE PERIOD

During the next block of Wait Time, my daughters and I had a coloring contest. Luckily, I had thought to bring Avery's Hello Kitty coloring book and crayons. I quickly discovered that whether you are four, seven, or thirty-nine years old, you never outgrow the love of coloring. All three of us became engrossed in our creations, occasionally exchanging crayons and complimenting each other's work. When the pictures were complete, they were so lovely that we declared them all first-place winners.

If I had chosen to spend that time looking at my phone, I would have missed this creative bonding experience with my daughters.

THE THIRD THIRTY-MINUTE PERIOD

During this segment of time, we simply talked. We discussed how Avery was soon going to kindergarten. Somehow this led to a lot of laughter about how much I would be crying that day!

We talked about Avery's swimming progress and her dreams of being on the swim team like her big sister. The topic of swimming then led to a very brief (and slightly disturbing) discussion about sharks.

We talked of summer plans to head north to see their adorable little cousin, Sam. Because of his obsession with farm equipment, this led to the longest discussion the girls ever had on John Deere tractors.

We talked about the upcoming spring concert and how Avery would delight her grandmother by singing "Amazing Grace" while strumming her ukulele.

If I had chosen to spend that time looking at my phone, I would have missed these priceless conversations that revealed my children's fears, dreams, hopes, and plans.

THE FOURTH THIRTY-MINUTE PERIOD

We spent the last block of Wait Time cuddling. Unexpectedly, Natalie curled up on my lap. She nestled her head in the crook of my neck and breathed a heavy sigh of anxiety. I couldn't recall the last time she sat on my lap for more than a few seconds. But in anticipation of seeing the doctor, my child needed the security of her mother's arms. As she rested against my chest, I whispered a prayer, asking God to give her strength and peace.

If I had chosen to spend that time looking at my phone, I would have missed an opportunity to comfort my child in her time of need.

Finally, after two hours, we were ushered into the exam room and the doctor arrived. He apologized for the wait, but I assured him we had made good use of our time.

After the exam, as I retrieved my phone to schedule our next appointment, it occurred to me that I had totally forgotten about my phone. Before my Hands Free journey, I couldn't imagine a two-hour wait without my phone. But now I know there is a much more valuable way to spend idle time.

Be with the loved one who sits beside you.

I felt a jolt of affirmation about the importance of choosing people over a phone when a preschool teacher in our online Hands Free community left this comment on my blog: "Last year around Mother's Day, I was helping students in my preschool class write about their moms for cards they were making. I asked each child to tell me what makes his or her mom special. One child's answer was about how much her mom loved her phone. That's what she said so that's what I helped her to write."

I ached for the child, but also for her mother. I knew all too well how a phone can become the primary focus of one's life despite the immense love a person has for her family. I prayed that the child's message provided the awareness the mother needed to curb her phone usage and reach for her child.

What we do while we wait with our children *does* matter. With each minute spent texting, surfing the Internet, checking social media, or reading emails, a chance to connect with our loved ones is lost. A chance to nurture our relationships is lost. A chance to make a memory is lost. A chance to be the parent our children want and need is lost.

Next time you have to wait, put the phone away. By doing so, idle time can become a gift to yourself and the ones you love.

HANDS FREE WEEKLY INTENTION

Turn Wait Time into Connection Time

The most powerful tactic I found for resisting device usage during Wait Time with my family members is to place temptation out of sight. Once we arrive at our destination, I zip my phone securely inside my purse. Keeping it out of sight greatly reduces my compulsion to check it.

This week, create a Connection Time activity bag with activities for your child to use next time you expect a wait.

- word search or activity books
- crayons and coloring books
- note cards and envelopes to write relatives
- a deck of playing cards
- sticky notes and colored pens
- small dolls or Matchbox cars
- a children's devotional
- Curiosity Cards that contain open-ended questions to spark discussion*

Using Wait Time to engage with the people you love could possibly be the most valuable use of idle time. Just think of the impact your choice will have on your children. You might very well be the only person in the waiting room not looking at a smartphone—and your children will reap the benefits—now and in the future.

---

*Curiosity Cards are available from rebeccaplants.com or amazon.com.

FULLY SUBMERGED

My younger daughter, Avery, recently learned to swim—really swim. I'm talking head under water, powerful kicks, and arms in stroke formation.

When I say this is *huge*, I mean it goes down on her list of

Momentous Achievements. It's right there with getting through the entire school day without sucking her thumb and bravely mastering the park's monstrous curly slide all by herself. You see, Avery spent three years of her life poolside watching her big sister collect enough swim-team ribbons to wallpaper her closet. Although Avery used swim-team lingo like "off the block" and "streamline" with proficiency and recognized a dolphin kick when she saw one, this little girl was terrified of the water.

But thanks to Miss Missy, a patient and skilled swim instructor, Avery overcame her fear and found she actually enjoyed the water! And now that she can swim, she wants to tell anyone who will listen. But she doesn't say, "I can swim." She says, "I can swim just like my big sister, Natalie."

The acquisition of this skill has resulted in her wanting to practice all the time. Not a day goes by that she doesn't beg me to take her swimming.

And Mother's Day was no exception.

To be honest, going to our gym's pool was not how I imagined spending my Mother's Day afternoon. So when Avery asked, I was tempted to suggest that both girls go with their father. He would have happily obliged. I envisioned myself relaxing in bed, cracking open one of those delicious books on my bedside table, and then taking a long, indulgent nap. Now *that* sounded like a perfect Mother's Day, if you ask me.

But my highly motivational yet sometimes inconveniently timed Hands Free inner voice had a very different opinion. It urged me to grasp what really mattered and go swimming with my family—but it didn't stop there. My very convincing Hands Free inner voice (that often doesn't know when to quit) suggested I do more than simply stand in the water watching, cheering, and clapping. It strongly recommended that I come off the sidelines, get into the action, and step right into the middle of the splash zone.

Translation: Actually swim and play in the water with my family.

There was only one small problem. I don't like to get my hair wet.

I know ... *lame.*

One of my dearest friends once described me as the perfect combination of tough and fancy. It's definitely the fancy part that doesn't like to get her hair wet. And since I'm stepping into the light of realness right now, I will admit I can't remember the last time I got my hair wet at the pool.

But on that Mother's Day afternoon, I had a choice. The difference between grasping what really mattered or letting it slip through my fingers depended on the choice I made. So I took a moment to evaluate the situation. I considered all the special things my family had done for me throughout the weekend to make me feel loved and appreciated. I noticed Avery's joyful face as she swam with a smile as big as her kicks. I marveled at the muscles in Natalie's arms as they effortlessly glided through the water. I watched Scott hoist the children high in the air and bring them down with a splash and an eruption of laughter.

It occurred to me that I was witnessing a moment in time that would never happen exactly this way again. And there was only one thing missing from this unforgettable, heartwarming scene — a scene that could one day become one of my children's favorite memories.

The only thing missing was me.

My family had given me so many wonderful gifts. Didn't they deserve my most precious gift — the gift of my time, focus, and attention? Because being fully present and active in the life of someone you love is the best gift anyone can offer. Going outside my comfort zone to step into *their* world is exactly the kind of gift my children are waiting to be given. Even if that means doing the dreaded 120-piece puzzle, learning more than I ever wanted to know about poisonous snakes, tossing the ball in overgrown grass, and yes, even getting my hair wet.

So in one spontaneous moment, I held my breath and jumped into the loving arms of my family.

I raced my daughter in freestyle — and became a victim of her contagious laughter as she beat me, not once, not twice, but three times.

I did somersaults until I was dizzy—and had to shake the water out of my ears just like I did as a kid.

I did an impressive cannonball from the side of the pool—and watched the amazed expression of two little girls who appeared to be thinking, "Wow! Mom is acting like a big kid!"

I held hands with my daughter as we dove to the bottom of the deep end—and then delighted in her description of a purple polka-dotted platypus she spotted in her imaginative play.

I floated on my back in the serenity of the water—and got lost in the peaceful underwater world that provided a momentary refuge from all that distracts and depletes me.

I found myself calling out, "Watch me!"

I was on a first-name basis with my kids who suddenly started referring to me as "Rachel."

I got my heart racing and my blood pumping.

I felt my hands become prunes.

I became light as a feather.

I felt stress leave my body.

I became fully submerged in the presence of my family.

And there was no other place I wanted to be.

On Mother's Day, I chose to get my hair wet. And in return, I was able to give and receive a gift I wouldn't have experienced any other way.

HANDS FREE WEEKLY INTENTION

Become Fully Submerged in the Passions of a Loved One

It saddens me to think about all the fun-loving opportunities I missed because I was holding tightly to my distractions. I always had an excuse about why I couldn't let loose and have fun:

- I'm too busy.
- I don't want to deal with the mess.

- I'm worried about what other people will think.
- It's too inconvenient.
- I feel insecure about my appearance.
- I'm afraid I won't be any good at it.
- I need to be productive—having fun is "slacking off."

A life-changing step in my journey was to let go of these restraints and become an active participant in my family's passions. Whatever initial fear or hesitation I had quickly dissolved the minute I saw how happy it made my family when I participated. They didn't care about my skill level, performance, or appearance—what mattered was my presence.

This week, set aside your distractions, reservations, and insecurities, and participate wholeheartedly in a loved one's activities. What are your children's passions and interests? What pastimes or hobbies does your spouse enjoy? When your loved one engages in a favorite activity, what do you do? Do you watch from the sidelines or are you an active participant? Do you retreat to your own comfortable domain when you could be creating a Sunset Moment? Here are some ideas of how you might keep company with your family while doing something they enjoy:

- Go on an insect hunt together with your child and marvel at the roly-poly you bravely hold in your hand.
- Play a round of golf with your dad.
- Act as kitchen assistant for the Easy-Bake Oven master chef.
- Take your hard-rocking ways to your wife's favorite country music concert.
- Watch a football game with your husband and cheer like a die-hard fan.

By placing your full and active presence within the passions and interests of a loved one, you offer yourself a chance to grasp what really matters. It is by immersing yourself in life's most beautiful moments with the people you love that you truly feel alive.

HANDS FREE REFLECTION

Deliberateness

You Choose Me

It used to be what you greeted first thing in the morning.
Now you greet me.
You say, "Good morning!" and "How did you sleep?"
Your hands, no longer clinging to the device, are available to hug me,
help me pour my cereal, and ruffle my hair.
Thank you for greeting me.

It used to be what you checked before bedtime.
Now you check me.
You make sure the covers are snug, the pages are turned,
and the monsters are shooed away.
Your voice and your presence, no longer given to someone on a screen,
remains on my skin as I drift off to sleep.
Thank you for checking me.

It used to be what you talked to for hours on end.
Now you talk to me.
You ask me about my dreams, my drawings,
my latest jokes, and darkest fears.
With your eyes you listen, really listen, no longer
summoned away by beeps and rings.
Thank you for talking to me.

It used to be what you held in your hand as you traveled room to room.
Now you hold me.
You hold me in your gaze, wrap me in your arms,
and take my hand in yours.
Your hands are free ... often leaving the devices behind ...
to cover me with love.
Thank you for holding me.

It used to be your favorite dinner companion, travel mate, and entertainer.
Now you seek me.
Your face beams at me through both your laughter and tears as
I show you all the things I can do and all the things I know.
You say, "Those other things can wait. Right now I am with you."
Thank you for seeking me.

I used to think you couldn't live without your electronic device.
But now I see there is something more important in your life.
It is me.
I am what you can't imagine life without.
I am what you can't bear to lose.
I am what holds your attention.
I am what illuminates your world.
You are choosing me.
And each time you do, I notice.
And my heart overflows with joy.
The phone is not so important anymore.
My childhood is not something you are willing to sacrifice.
Thank you for choosing me.

REFLECTION QUESTIONS

When you are in situations where you have to wait (stoplights, restaurants, sporting events), do you reach for your device? What factors might you consider before looking at the phone to help you choose human connection instead?

What small moments in the daily routine are you using to engage in human connection instead of digital distraction? What positive differences are you seeing?

Reflect on a time in the past week when you chose to let go of distraction and grasp a moment that mattered. What helped you make that choice?

Chapter 4

RECOGNIZE THE GIFT OF TODAY

Presentness

One day at a time—this is enough. Do not look back and grieve over the past for it is gone; and do not be troubled about the future, for it has not yet come. Live in the present, and make it so beautiful it will be worth remembering.

Ida Scott Taylor

WHEN I WAS LIVING DISTRACTED, I took time for granted. It was as if I had some magical power that guaranteed time would never run out. So I continually put things off—not my "urgent" daily tasks like phone calls, emails, thank-you notes, and cleaning duties. No, I put off the important things. "When I get this project finished, I'll spend time with the family" or "When I get caught up, we'll do something fun together" were just a few of the empty promises I rattled off with ease. I probably would have continued to postpone living had it not been for this undeniable reality: there was always another project; there was no catching up; there was no slowing down. But all of that changed when I began to recognize the gift of today.

As I progressed through my Hands Free journey, I became acutely aware of the value of *now*. I realized that phrases like "maybe later" and "in a minute" didn't just cost a few precious seconds; they cost me a future—a future relationship with the people I loved and precious future memories of time spent together. Through daily moments of meaningful connection, I realized that the memories my children and I would someday cherish were made in the mundane, everyday moments of daily life—chatting while waiting for the bus, laughing as she helped me make dinner, and snuggling as she watched her favorite television show.

This next step marked the end of empty promises. No longer would I bank on family vacations and holidays to invest time in relationships and create memories. It was the beginning of living, laughing, and loving every single day I was blessed to be alive.

We need constant reminders about the importance of grasping daily opportunities to make meaningful connections and create lasting memories. I hope the stories in this chapter will inspire you to nurture relationships, create family traditions, and build lasting memories throughout the daily routines of life.

CONSIDER YOURSELF GIFTED

Avery wandered into the kitchen clutching her stuffed bunny in one hand, sucking her thumb on the other hand. As I buttered toast, I expected her to grasp my leg and rest her cheek against my thigh. But today she offered something more. Although there had been a time in my life when I would have been too busy or too distracted to see it, I didn't miss it today.

I got it before one more email, one more text message, and one more yes to an unnecessary commitment stole another precious moment.

I got it before one more "after I fold this load of laundry" or one more "after I clean up the playroom" denied me another one of life's simple joys.

I got it before one more "when I lose five more pounds" or

one more "what will people think?" prevented me from dancing, laughing, and truly living.

I got it before one more empty, shallow, and meaningless distraction robbed me of one more glorious experience that makes life worth living.

And because I finally got it, I saw a chance to grasp what really matters. Beneath me stood my beautiful child who had suddenly dropped her pink bunny and stopped sucking her thumb so she could hold up her arms to me—just like she did when she was a baby.

For a moment, I froze. I couldn't remember the last time she'd wanted me to pick her up. There had been many fragmented and sleepless nights that claimed precious brain cells between those days and now. I hadn't expected this. I thought the "hold me" days had passed, like the way she had stopped shortening her sister's name to "Na Na." I couldn't pinpoint the day it happened—I just knew when it was gone.

Although I was still a Hands Free work-in-progress—still occasionally unable to slow down and surrender control—I knew a golden opportunity when I saw it. And there was one standing beneath me in fuzzy pink polka-dotted pajamas.

I turned away from the burning toast, the unmade school lunches, and the unsigned homework folders. I turned away from distraction and toward what, or *who*, really mattered. I opened my arms and scooped her up—just like I did when she was a baby. Although her gangly arms and legs felt awkward as they wrapped around my neck and waist, her head still fit perfectly in the crook of my neck. She nuzzled in. This little girl planned to stay for a while.

In that moment I made a vow. No matter what happens around me, no matter what I feel I need to do, I will never be the first to let go. I breathed deeply into her hair. The scent of a girl who doesn't like to wash her hair fueled a barrage of memories like oxygen to my lungs ... the way she once caressed her nose as she sucked her baby-sized thumb ... the way she adeptly walked on her knees until she was nearly two years old ... the way her three-year-old fingers strummed her ukulele in time with her pretty singing voice.

With each passing minute inside this brilliant kaleidoscope of memories, her forty-pound body became lighter and lighter in the cradle of my arms. As I stood there swaying with my precious child, I recalled the painful words a reader had left on my blog:

> I am now in my sixties. I wish I had known then what I know now. I lost a lot of opportunities with my children and the people I love because I was busy doing things I thought were "important." My current relationship with my children is okay, but I can only imagine what it would be like now if I had spent more time with them, talking to them, and laughing with them. I think they managed to have those meaningful experiences in life, but it wasn't with me. Tell your readers that the cost of distraction is mighty high. It can cost you your life and your happiness. Take it from someone who knows.

I think this dear woman would understand why I thanked God at that moment for opening my eyes before my future contained the same regrets. As I hugged my child's body tighter, I marveled at this God-given revelation that seemed almost too good to be true:

I have today. Yesterday is gone. All the mistakes, failures, poor choices, and the things I wish I could do over, they are gone.

Today stands before me with arms wide open.

All I have to do is grasp it.

 ## HANDS FREE WEEKLY INTENTION

Take Time to Pause for What's Important

During my distracted years, I thought stopping in the midst of my busy schedule would throw off the entire day. But when I began to pause—even for a minute—to look my child in the eyes when she spoke, marvel at her artistic creations, or help locate her favorite boots, I immediately noticed a positive change in behavior. Stopping for a moment to offer my undivided

attention to my children, as well as my spouse, improved our home environment and impacted everyone's attitudes. My family began to offer me the
same kindness and respect when I spoke or needed something from them.
These brief moments of mindful connection improved our interactions so
that there was greater opportunity for bonding and memory-making each
day. My children were also more patient in times when they had to wait for
my attention because I was making the effort to stop when I was able.

This week, when your child or loved one speaks to you or asks you
to do something, instead of saying, "In a minute," offer a moment of your
time right then.

Even sixty seconds of undivided attention can have a positive impact
on the behavior and atmosphere in your home. Taking these intentional
pauses throughout the day will not only strengthen your relationships, but
also allow time to make a memory.

THE PRESENT THAT IS YOUR PAST

I opened my mailbox to find a small, square envelope with my
name hand-printed on the front. Sandwiched between a stack
of business envelopes, this pastel-colored gem brought me a tiny
surge of joy.

As I removed the card, I thought it might be a baby announcement or a party invitation. In this case, it was a thank-you note
for a memorial contribution I sent as an expression of sympathy.
Typically, I love to read notes of gratitude and appreciation, but
not this time. The content of the note was lovely and meaningful,
but I didn't feel warm and fuzzy inside.

I got stuck on one sentence.

This particular sentence struck me with the undeniable reality that a person can go from present to past—just like that. The
fragility of life was etched in blue ballpoint pen. It read, "My sister
would have loved you."

Would have . . .

The note didn't say, "My sister *is going to* love you," nor did it say, "My sister *will* love you," because that opportunity was now gone. A young, vibrant mother was taken too soon, and her life had left an irreplaceable hole.

As I tucked the note into a drawer, I was preoccupied by the thought of dying—not dying people, but dying moments.

I know that *this moment*, the one I am currently in *right now*, will become my past, but seldom do I treat these precious minutes as I should. I often fail to realize that if I use these mundane, ordinary passing seconds engaging in something that matters, they will eventually add up to a past that mattered. For it is in the everyday moments, doing routine activities, that we create the past.

Let me put it this way.

The sit-down dinner you shared with your family last night and the night before that and the night before that—that is now your past.

The silly wake-up routine you've had with your child every single morning since he was small whether you felt like it or not—that is now your past.

The trip to the farmer's market you've taken with your family every single Saturday since it opened—that is now your past.

The time of conversation and connection you had with your spouse last Friday night—that is now your past.

The daily and weekly rituals of your life add up. Not only do they create *your* past, but they quite possibly also create the past of someone you love. What you choose to do with those moments, in addition to the value you place on them, can mean the difference in creating lasting memories or creating none at all.

We can't see the future. We can't predict how all those special nightly tuck-ins or family traditions are going to add up . . . or can we? Recently, I felt as if I had a glimpse into my future. And this awareness profoundly changed the way I regard my everyday routines.

My glimpse came courtesy of a blog reader with children much older than my own. Her story beautifully illustrates how minutes spent actively participating in a daily routine can eventually add up to something significant:

> Long ago, my husband and I chose to live fifty minutes from the city in which we work. This meant 110 minutes in the car with my daughter every single day throughout her school years.
>
> It would have been easy for me to look at the tiresome and difficult drive to school, church, and all civilization for that matter, as a dreaded inconvenience. But I didn't.
>
> I could have reasoned that by using that travel time to handle work-related phone calls or email messages, I would have less to do when I got home. But I didn't.
>
> Instead, I have viewed this daily drive as my opportunity to connect [with] and understand my daughter. While in the confines of our vehicle, she is a captive audience for me and I am for her. It is there that we share special talks, have meaningful connections, private jokes and heart-to-heart chats. Each time we ride together, I hear the important happenings of her day.
>
> What has resulted from this routine, daily activity is a wonderful foundation for our mother/daughter bond. I know if I had not committed to being fully present during these long drives, I would not know the child I am preparing to send to college next year nearly as well as I do.

My friend, here's the bottom line:

The time you spend with your family around the dinner table adds up.

The time you spend tucking in your child in bed at night adds up.

The time you spend talking to the one you love adds up.

The time you spend writing, painting, sewing, constructing, or pursuing your dream adds up.

Because how you choose to spend that ten minutes in the car, that extra hour of time in the evening, that last twenty minutes of your child's day—it *all* adds up. And twenty years from now those minutes can add up to *nothing* or they can add up to *something that matters.*

HANDS FREE WEEKLY INTENTION

Start a Simple Family Tradition

When I began my Hands Free journey, I made it my goal to do one memorable activity every weekend. I stopped making excuses for not investing at least a fraction of our weekend time in the people and activities I cherish. I quickly found that whether the activity was free or required money, whether it lasted an hour or a whole day, simply announcing that we were doing something special as a family set the stage for bonding and happiness.

Choose a recurring activity or simple family tradition you could start this weekend. For example:

- family game night
- a memorable bedtime routine like bedtime stories and snuggles, piggyback rides to bed, or sharing your own childhood memories
- "Learn Something New" weekend tradition, like how to grow an herb garden, how to do a cartwheel, how to play a few chords on a guitar, or how to juggle
- dinner-time conversation starters like word of the day, highs and lows, or saying what each member of the family is thankful for

Our family's most treasured ritual is nightly Talk Time, which was started by my older daughter when she was a toddler. In the soft glow of the nightlight, Natalie voiced dreams of being a teacher and revealed that she was being bullied. Wrapped in the warmth of a blanket, she asked questions about heaven, life, and falling in love. Talk Time minutes are the best minutes I spend each day. No matter how tired, stressed, or distracted I am going in, I come out feeling connected, peaceful, and renewed. It costs me ten minutes, but the payoff is huge. I am privy to the topics on my children's hearts and minds. Something tells me I may be even more grateful in ten years when I see the beautiful results of this daily ritual.

The time you invest in the people you love will always add up to something that matters. Not only will these traditions positively impact your life today, but also tomorrow and in the years to come.

A WELL-LOVED CHILD

For two whole days my husband and I were able to postpone telling Natalie that her beloved pink Dog Dog was left behind in a tidal wave of hotel bed sheets, hastily forgotten in a rushed early morning departure.

It didn't help that my daughter has humongous brown eyes, like succulent chocolate pools in which I can easily drown. That night, I could barely stand to look at them. They were framed by wet eyelashes and clouded with despair. And they were looking to me for hope.

"Will Dog Dog come back, Mama?" she asked as prominent tears made glistening trails upon her flushed cheeks.

I felt guilty even suggesting there was a chance Dog Dog might return, but I took the easy way out. "We have left several messages, and I am praying we hear something tomorrow." My voice faltered, yet my emotion went unnoticed as my child grasped this tidbit of hope like a life preserver that suddenly popped out of nowhere. She threw her entire body onto it and clung with all her might.

"I bet we'll get good news tomorrow, Mama," she whispered, now slightly more composed than in the heartbreaking minutes before.

Thankfully, I had gotten my own cry out two nights before when I read the email my husband wrote to the management where we stayed. The line that got me was this one: "In room #556, our child left behind her stuffed dog that she has slept with since she was born." Those words literally made my heart stop for one brief moment. I could envision my daughter holding that special plush toy at every phase of life from six months to eight years. As soon as she learned to grasp something in her hand, Dog Dog was carried everywhere—as if divinely superglued to her hand. With each passing year, her constant companion lost a little more fur and became a little less pink. His middle section became limp from being squeezed in her bionic grip as he was toted from place to place. His tag was lovingly rubbed down to a nub between two chubby fingers.

In other words, he showed signs of being well loved.

Year after year, I watched my child sleep with her beloved critter as close to her face as her own breath. I'm so grateful I watched her sleep the night before Dog Dog was so carelessly left behind. His floppy, furless body was positioned right under my daughter's nose where she had nestled him for most of her life. As she slept, she inhaled his scent, smiling as if she dreamed of endless summer days and bottomless hot fudge sundaes. I briefly wondered when Natalie would decide she was too big to sleep with Dog Dog. She had once mentioned planning to preserve him in a box in her closet when she got older so she could show him to her own child someday. I knew the day would come when she no longer needed to sleep with her precious toy, but this was not the way I had imagined it would happen. No, not this way. Not this rip-your-heart-out kind of way that has the brutal finality of an unexpected loss.

As my child lay wide awake in bed, wondering if she would ever see her stuffed companion again, my hands couldn't help but write the painfully valuable message that flowed from my fingers and escaped through my tears. The lesson of the little pink dog is a powerful one. If you love a child, brace yourself. This poem delves into painful territory that we seldom allow our minds and hearts to tread.*

THERE WILL COME A DAY . . .

There will come a day when she no longer wants to hold my
  hand.
So I will hold it while I still can.
There will come a day when she no longer tells me what's on
  her mind.
So I will listen while she still wants to talk to me.
There will come a day when she no longer says, "Watch me,
  Mama!"

Update: Shortly after writing this story, Dog Dog was discovered by the hotel housekeeping service. A true angel named Narciso recognized Dog Dog as a child's beloved companion that had been terribly misplaced. Dog Dog traveled great distances to be reunited with Natalie—and he hasn't left the house since.

So I will observe and encourage while I still can.
There will come a day when she no longer invites me to eat
school lunch with her.
So I will join her while I still can.
There will come a day when she no longer needs my help to
bake cookies or hit the tennis ball in the sweet spot.
So I will stand beside her gently guiding and instructing while I still can.
There will come a day when she no longer wants my opinion
about clothes, friendship, death, and heaven.
So I will share my views while she still wants to hear them.
There will come a day when she no longer allows me to hear
her prayers and her dreams.
So I will fold my hands and absorb every word while I still can.
There will come a day when she no longer sleeps with her
beloved stuffed animal.
And that day may come sooner than I think.
Because sometimes unexpected events happen, causing the
days to rush by, the years to tumble ahead.
Sometimes what I thought I would have time to do,
Like listen to her laugh,
Wipe her tears,
Breathe her scent,
And hold her close,
Will no longer be available to me.
What I thought I had all the time in the world to do,
May no longer be an option.
The little pink dog that my child must now learn to sleep
without after eight precious years reminds me that tomor-
row may not allow for all the things I planned to do.
So instead of being too busy,
Too tired,
Or too distracted when she seeks my love and attention,
I will be ready and waiting
To make her a well-loved child
While I still can.

HANDS FREE WEEKLY INTENTION

Speak Words of Love

One of the most impactful gems I received on my Hands Free journey came from an article called "Three Things to Say to Your Child Every Day" by Lisa A. McCrohan, Wellness Counselor at Georgetown University.* She explains the power of these three phrases:

> *I see you.*
> *You matter.*
> *I love to watch you.*

"When spoken and repeated every day," she writes, "these messages begin to take up residence in a little one's soul. He begins to believe in his worth. She begins to carry these messages with her. He learns how to see others. She learns how to love herself and others . . . just from a few simple moments of pausing and seeing our kiddos. Repeated. Every day."

Incorporate one or more of the three loving phrases in your daily interactions with your children. Small phrases, when accompanied by the gift of our presence, can make a significant impact on our most precious relationships.

*Lisa A. McCrohan, "Three Things to Say to Your Child Every Day," *Gems of Delight*, barefootbarn.wordpress.com/2013/07/02/three-things-to-say-to-your-child-every-day/ (July 2, 2013).

XO BEFORE YOU GO

Are there times when you suddenly realize that something you used to do for your child or grandchild is no longer needed? Like when you are no longer needed to hold him or her up to get a drink at a certain water fountain. Or how the step stool he or she used to help you in the kitchen is no longer required. The worst is when that word she couldn't say correctly for the longest time (at our house it was "hanitizer" instead of "hand sanitizer" and "errupting" instead of "interrupting") now slides off her tongue with perfect pronunciation.

When that moment of realization hits, I feel as if I've been punched in the gut. It's a miniature loss. When such realizations occur, I experience a brief period of mourning, knowing there will never again be another "funder storm" or another backward *s*.

I became aware of one such loss as I waited to pick up my kindergartener in the carpool line one afternoon. On this particular day I could hardly wait to see her. For some reason, I was longing to hold her.

And then it hit me — one of those miniature losses.

Throughout the first several months of kindergarten it was a tradition, a daily ritual, for us to exchange a hug and kiss before she got into the car to go to school. For three solid months Avery never left without this loving exchange.

Suddenly I realized it didn't happen anymore.

I racked my brain ... when had it stopped?

I felt ashamed because I didn't know.

All I knew was that now my little girl just hopped into our friend's vehicle every morning with a smile and a quick "I love you, Mama!"

I'm sure you might be thinking, "Actually, that is *good*. That is what you want your child to do — to become independent."

I would agree ... *except* ... I'm on a journey to grasp the moments that matter. And a hug and kiss before you leave the company of someone you love is at the top of my official Moments That Matter list. In fact, it just *might* hold the number-one position of what really matters in my life.

I had a sneaking suspicion that my child still needed, welcomed, and treasured a morning goodbye hug and kiss, but the tradition had just gotten lost in the chaotic morning rush.

Daily distraction strikes again.

Well, I wanted the tradition back.

And I had the power to make it happen.

Immediately, I thought of the parents who didn't have the power to make it happen, and I couldn't help but cry for them. Whenever I see a story of such tragic loss, I force myself to read the heartbreaking stories from beginning to end. I need those powerful reminders; I need to be shaken with the realization that there could be a day when my child walks out that door and never walks back in. God forbid it would occur on a day that I didn't give her a hug and kiss goodbye.

So when Avery and I cuddled at bedtime, I immediately confessed I had been feeling badly about something. "Remember how you used to *always* give me a hug and kiss before you went to school each morning?" I asked.

She nodded solemnly and I continued.

"Well, now you just hop in the car and wave goodbye with no hug and kiss. And I think it might be because I am so focused on homework, backpack, lunch, snack, shoes, socks, and hair that it gets forgotten."

Her expression now matched my own: sadness.

I pulled her onto my lap and whispered, "I don't want it to be like that anymore. I don't want you to leave without a hug and kiss before you go each morning. Would that be okay with you?"

Avery barely waited until I finished my sentence when an exuberant yes came out of her mouth. Then my clever little kindergartener, who grew up seeing colorful sticky notes plastered to our microwave, doorknobs, and countertops, quickly offered up a way to remember. She reached for her journal, flipped to a clean page, and started writing. Within minutes, the reminder sign read: *XOXO Before You Go*. The motto was brilliant—and it even rhymed! This was my singin', ukulele-playin' child all right.

The next morning, the *XO* sign was fresh on my daughter's mind. She ran right over to the door leading to the garage to make sure I had placed it exactly where she instructed. When she saw it, she smiled so widely that her eyes became all crinkly—

that is when I knew I had hit the bull's-eye on grasping what really matters.

Before long, we were doing the morning scramble to gather shoes, coats, and book bags. But today I had something else on my mind. And it was taking priority over the not-as-important details. I called out, "We can't forget *XOXO Before You Go!*"

Natalie, who was standing there ready to exit, raised her eyebrows and asked, "What is *that*?"

My kindergartner responded by happily demonstrating. She ran into my arms and hugged me with all her strength and then kissed me tenderly on the cheek.

Although my older daughter had a "you-guys-are-weird" look on her face, I grabbed her and kissed her too. She actually melted into me for several seconds. I swear she breathed my scent like an old familiar friend who had been sorely missed. The Hands Free reminders often come when I least expect them—but I don't need to be told twice.

Minutes later, we pulled up to the carpool line at school. Avery was the last to exit, behind Natalie and two friends. "XO Before You Go!" she hollered as a pair of soft pink lips planted one more kiss on my cheek without warning.

I had begun this day seeking *one* kiss and *one* hug. I ended up getting three—and so much more. What mattered most was now as close as a breath upon on my face.

My cheek tingled on the spot where I'd been kissed. I hoped it might remain there all day.

I placed my hand softly over the warm spot on my face and thanked God for this beautiful reminder: Although I cannot control what happens once they leave my side, I can control what happens in those sacred minutes before we say goodbye.

 ## HANDS FREE WEEKLY INTENTION

Without Fail, Give a Proper Goodbye

At the height of my distracted life, it required a near tragedy for me to slow down and tell my family exactly why I love them. Now that I am on my Hands Free journey, I have discovered that in the minute or two that it takes to create a sign of love, I experience the most beautiful feeling of peace and gratitude.

Do what you need to do to allow yourself sixty extra seconds for an unrushed, undivided, loving goodbye.

- Have your child make a reminder sign so it's not forgotten in the morning rush.
- Get organized for departure the night before (pack lunches, complete homework, lay out clothes, and so on).
- Refrain from logging onto the computer until after your children leave for school.

If you can only make one small effort to let go of distraction and grasp what matters in a day, do this—avoid being distracted when your child or loved one leaves your presence. Regardless of where they are going or how long they will be gone, let them know they are loved and will be missed. Life is unpredictable. Make the most of every goodbye.

HANDS FREE REFLECTION

Presentness

Today Let Me Appreciate ...

I fail to appreciate the feeling of her small body in footy pajamas until she suddenly outgrows them and declares, "I want regular pajamas—ones that don't have feet."

Today let me appreciate the perfect size and shape she is right now, today, in this moment.

Today let me appreciate my child.

I fail to appreciate those odd mannerisms that drive me crazy until we are separated for a time, and suddenly I long to hear one of those silly quirks.

Today let me appreciate the gum chewing, the knuckle cracking, and even the humming, because when I hear these things I know I am in the company of my love.

Today let me appreciate my husband.

I fail to appreciate the richness of my life until I walk down the busy street and see sadness on the fringes—those with empty hands, empty eyes, and empty souls.

Today let me appreciate the fact that I have known love in my life and let me share it with one who has not.

Today let me appreciate the value of spreading kindness.

I fail to appreciate the wrinkles, the bulges, and the sags until I reflect on all that I have endured to be where I am today.

Today let me appreciate each beautiful memory of my life that is etched across my face and body.

Today let me appreciate the positive value of growing older.

Today let me appreciate the sun—even when it's behind the clouds.

Today let me appreciate the goodbyes—even if it's not our last.

Today let me appreciate the goodness—even if I have to dig a little to find it.

> Today let me appreciate the gifts in the mundane, ordinary moments that are graciously given to me. Because even though they're far from perfect ... and sometimes they're messy and hard ... these are the moments that make up a lifetime.
>
> And for this *anything-but-small* miracle that is my life, I am thankful.

REFLECTION QUESTIONS

Do you put off spending time with loved ones or delay doing things you enjoy until certain duties are complete and you have "more time"? Does that ideal moment ever arrive?

What daily or weekly rituals are special to your family? How do they make you feel connected to the sacred parts of your life? What actions will you take this week to protect these rituals or begin new ones?

Chapter 5

TAKE PAUSE

Serenity

There is more to life than simply increasing its speed.
Mahatma Gandhi

MIDWAY THROUGH MY JOURNEY, it occurred to me why my distracted life had been so exhausting. For two long years, there had only been one speed: full throttle. The two words I said most often were *hurry up*. There was always somewhere to go, something to do, and never enough time to do it. Whenever I did finally sit down, my family thought I was sick. Only injury or illness could bring my body to a complete stop.

Perhaps that is why this next step was so momentous. It was sparked one day as I waited for my child to emerge from preschool. Instead of looking at my phone's screen or checking my to-do list, I simply watched for her. When my child saw me, her eyes creased into tiny, joyful slivers that seem to merge with the upturned corners of her mouth. She vigorously waved her chubby hand as if she were greeting Mickey Mouse himself. As I waved back, tears began to flow. *Oh, dear God, I didn't know anyone could be this happy to see me*—because I hadn't stopped long enough to notice. From that moment, I vowed not to miss the hellos, the goodbyes, or the other beautiful exchanges that got lost in my harried wake.

To do this, I had to dismiss my inner drill sergeant. What was the point in having a long list of superficial things accomplished if I missed my children's precious smiles and tender words in the process? Immediately, I experienced the benefits of taking time to simply *be*. There were more loving words, more cuddles, and more smiles. I was no longer an untouchable blur whizzing from point A to point B in nanoseconds. I was available to give and receive love in the sacred pauses of a busy day.

On the Hands Free journey, it's essential to assess the high cost of living overly wired, overly scheduled, hurried, and stressed. The stories and intentions in this chapter offer insights to help you adopt new practices for waiting, resting, relaxing, playing, and connecting with the treasured people in your life.

HAPPY TO SEE ME

For several summers during college I worked in day care. My favorite part of the job was the end of the day when I got to present the babies to their parents at pick-up time. As two sets of eyes locked, I could see and feel a spontaneous surge of joy between parent and child. I looked forward to the day when I had a child of my own so I could experience what appeared to be one of the highlights of parenthood.

These experiences came to mind years later when my young nephew started day care—his pick-up time was all I could think about that day. Later, I listened intently as my sister-in-law gave me a play-by-play of their joyful reunion. Through her detailed description, I envisioned my adorable nephew with his salon-worthy locks reaching out his dimpled hands toward the woman who rocked his world. Drool oozed from his toothless smile as he practically jumped into his mother's arms.

I can say with certainty that my sister-in-law started collecting hellos at that moment and so did my nephew. *Collecting hellos* means memorizing the joyful expression upon a loved one's face when united after a separation. These mental snapshots become a sacred collection that can provide comfort when faced with the pain of long-term goodbyes.

My sister-in-law thought about her son every single minute of that dreadfully long first day and couldn't wait to retrieve him. When I thought of what her smile might have looked like when they reunited, the words *Sun Delay* came to mind. *Sun Delay* is a term used in traffic reports when the glare of the sun is so strong that drivers have difficulty seeing the road. Traffic slows because the sun is so bright.

When my nephew was lifted into his mother's arms, the world slowed down. His mother's smile was all he could see. And knowing the kind of mother my sister-in-law is, I speculated that her greeting on his first day of day care was just the first of many Sun-Delay greetings in his lifetime.

But this got me thinking.

What about my own children? As a day-care worker, I longed to experience the loving reunion between parent and child. Yet as my children's needs have decreased and the twenty-first-century distractions have increased, the loving greetings have fallen along the wayside.

Sometimes I don't look away from the computer screen when my child walks into the room.

Sometimes I pick up my children from extracurricular events or school while talking on the phone.

Sometimes the first thing my child sees in the morning is not my smiling face, but the top of my head as I send email messages or the back of my head while I watch the morning news.

The truth hurts, but the truth heals—and brings me closer to the parent I want to be.

Even as a twenty-year-old college student, I recognized the importance of a deliberate hello. Perhaps that was because a loving, intentional greeting was a constant in my own formative years. Despite the fact that at times I was a difficult child, teenager, and young adult, my mom's greeting never changed. No matter what, she was always happy to see me. And even though I acted annoyed and didn't always return the love, I cherished my mother's greetings. In fact, I *counted* on them. Knowing I brought that look of happiness to my mother's face inexplicably saved me a time or two. In the midst of some very hard rains, my mother's hellos were rays of sunshine on my hopeless soul.

I don't want my children to grow up without loving hellos. I vow to let go of my distractions long enough to cause a Sun Delay:

No matter what I am in the middle of doing,
No matter how inconvenient it is to look up,
No matter how busy I think I am,
When my children walk in the room,
When my children hop in the car,
When my children and I are reunited after a separation,
The world is going to stop for a moment.
And I will shine my love into their eyes and into their hearts,
So my children *see* and *feel* how much I love them.

 **HANDS FREE WEEKLY INTENTION**

Create a Sun Delay

Making a concerted effort to offer my full attention when greeting my loved ones was a turning point in my journey. I found that it didn't take much effort to set aside my distractions when reuniting with my child or spouse after a separation, yet the impact was immeasurable.

A highly achievable approach to living Hands Free is to offer your undivided attention during a few specific times of day. Parenting expert Janet Lansbury suggests three times when our attention is most desired by our children:

- when we reconnect after a separation
- when our children are performing or exerting themselves (like on the soccer field)
- during meals

> Lansbury writes, "When parents text on the car ride home, check email at the soccer game, or are glued to their laptops during social or intimate activities like mealtimes, they aren't providing the connectivity a child needs."*
>
> Saying "I love you" is easy, but showing love—that takes effort. It can't be faked. It can only be genuinely achieved when you push away distraction, if only for a moment, and focus on that God-given gift that stands before you.
>
> Choose one of the three times of day listed above to offer your loved one undivided attention. When parents greet their children with excitement, interest, and warmth, the message they convey is: *you are loved*. It is my belief that greeting our children with happiness and love matters more than any other parental effort we can make.
>
> ---
>
> *Janet Lansbury, "Do Wired Parents Need More Time Out ... or Less Guilt?" *janetlansbury.com*, janetlansbury.com/2010/06/do-wired-parents-need-time-out-or-less-guilt/ (June 25, 2010).

ARE YOU AVAILABLE?

When my daughter received the DVD boxed set of *Little House on the Prairie* for her birthday, I was nearly as excited as she was. Some of my fondest childhood memories involve cuddling with my family as life in Walnut Grove played out on a static-lined television screen.

Yet when I looked at the discs and realized there were forty-four *Little House* episodes, my first thoughts were very Non–Hands Free. I looked at that collection of DVDs and saw forty-four opportunities to be otherwise highly productive.

Although my inner drill sergeant doesn't hold as much authority as it once did, that demanding voice of productivity and efficiency still tries to tempt me to the other side—straight into the arms of distraction. *Just think how much you could get accomplished while the girls watch* Little House. *They will not make a peep for the entire fifty-minute episode, and in that time you could easily knock several items off your to-do list!*

But my Hands Free inner voice gently reminded me about what really mattered. *This is your chance to sit your constantly moving body down on the couch, hold your daughters, and be a part of their world. Don't blow it.*

So after dinner the following Friday night, we put on our pajamas, popped popcorn, grabbed the softest blankets we own, and pushed the Play button on episode one, "A Harvest of Friends."

I was the first to find a spot on the couch. And just as my backside hit the leather, my two children drew to my sides as if they were being sucked toward me by the world's most powerful magnet. One child magnetized to my left, the other to my right. Not even the tiniest popcorn kernel, should it fall from our hands, could come between this solid mass of togetherness.

Sit on the couch much, Rachel Stafford?

I decided this was not the time to berate myself for not doing more couch time with my children. It was time to enjoy *this* moment, the one I chose over dishes, laundry, writing, cleaning, emailing, or multitasking all five activities at once. I had gotten *this* choice right.

And I got the following forty-three consecutive episodes right too.

I stayed true to the promise I made myself. *Little House* means family time, and my children are fully aware and delighted that we do this together. For that fifty-minute period, I am not a moving target that my daughters have .01 percent chance of hitting. Instead, I am available to sit there and simply love them.

I don't really like to think about it too much, but my older child will only live in my house for ten more years. Ten years. That's nothing—the blink of an eye.

And if I continue darting about the house, going from one activity to the next for the remaining ten years, I can be sure of one thing: I will not hear my children's thoughts, questions, revelations, troubles, or triumphs.

Because here's some reality:

No child wants to talk to the back of a parent's head.

No child wants to make an appointment to get a little of a parent's time.

No child wants to talk to a parent who can't look up from distraction long enough to make eye contact.

Thanks to an experience shared by a blog reader, I've been given some insight about what children *do* want from a parent.

> My eighteen-year-old son who left for college in August called me on Sunday night. After we had the "How are classes going?" conversation, the "How much money is in your account?" conversation, and the "Do you have any clean laundry?" conversation, he said, "I really miss you, Mom."
>
> I was thinking, *Yes, I'm sure you do miss me—washing clothes and making dinner.*
>
> It was then that I asked him, "Oh, yeah, what do you miss about Mom?"
>
> His answer was simple, but it stunned me.
>
> "I miss just talking to you. You know, at the end of the day, when we were both home … I miss talking to you."
>
> Before I knew it, I was crying. Of all the things I had done for him as his mom, the thing he missed the most was talking to me.

A few days after reading this, I was gathering activities for Avery to do while we sat at Natalie's swim meet. Normally I would have packed my writing folder, but it struck me that maybe this was not an opportunity to check something off the list … maybe this was an opportunity to *be available*.

I left my work at home and instead brought a few of my daughter's favorite books and a snack to share. Avery spent a lot of the time just sitting on my lap—a lap that, for once, was empty. We had the most wonderful conversation and snuggle time.

As my legs grew numb under the weight of her body, she turned to me and said nine of the most blessed words I have heard since beginning my journey to live Hands Free.

"This is the kind of mom I always wanted."

By "this" I knew exactly what she meant.

Present
Attentive
Still
Available
Available

Completely available to love her.

 **HANDS FREE WEEKLY INTENTION**

Engage in Do-Nothing Moments

To take this step in the journey, I had to change my mind-set. For far too long, I believed that activities with no end product were a waste of time. But then I witnessed something magical happen when I simply plopped down in the places where my children congregated. My children drew close to me like magnets. It was in these Do-Nothing Moments with no agenda and no itinerary that I heard the tender conversations going on in their hearts and minds. Suddenly, there was great value in pausing—in fact, getting to know my children in these moments was and is a priceless gift.

Have a Do-Nothing Moment:

- cuddle together
- take a walk (let the child set the pace)
- place your ear on the chest of a loved one and listen to his or her heartbeat
- sit outside and observe nature
- watch your child play

By routinely making yourself available to the people who matter to you, you offer a dependable and constant source of love and support. When faced with moments of joy and uncertainty, your loved ones will know right where to find you.

WAITING JOYFULLY

Recently Avery and I were on our way to school when I noticed the time. We were running late because she had decided at the last minute to use the bathroom, add a sparkly accessory to her ensemble, and locate her favorite pair of furry boots.

There was a time not too long ago when being late would have stressed me out. But on this beautiful day, I continued driving at the speed limit, chatting with my daughter about a marshmallow letter project she completed in school the day before.

It is in moments like these that I catch myself and think *I can't believe this is me. I love being Hands Free Rachel.* Now don't get me wrong, I would still classify myself as a Hands Free work in progress—but I am making progress, and this gives me hope.

A few minutes later, we were parked in the school lot. I turned to look at my daughter and watched as she unbuckled herself and then confidently began to strap her beloved Froggy into her booster seat. Avery had recently mastered the seat belt–buckling skill and was struggling to hear the magic click. Deep in concentration, my child's pink tongue was sticking out of the corner of her mouth.

By this time, she was more than a couple minutes late for school. I looked into the rearview mirror and was about to say, "Come on, we gotta go," but something stopped me.

I didn't say a word. I decided to wait.

I saw the way my daughter was so determined to get her Froggy buckled in. Her little fingers pushed the buckle this way and that way. Miraculously, she wasn't becoming frustrated, only more determined. I was tempted to ask her if she needed help. Again, I refrained and waited.

It was then that Avery spoke the most precious words to her stuffed frog. As she diligently worked on that uncooperative buckle, she whispered in a hushed, soothing voice, "Once I put you in your place, Froggy, you'll be fine. You'll be just fine, Froggy." Then she added, "You'll be super fine."

And then I heard the happy click of the seat belt.

My curly-haired child then said goodbye to her well-loved toy lazily slouching in the oversized booster seat. Now my child was ready to go.

After getting Avery settled in class, I came out and sat in my car for a moment. I felt a surge of gratitude that I hadn't rushed my daughter that morning. There were two opportunities when I could have hurried her along. But instead, I waited patiently. I waited as one does for a festive event or special occasion: I waited joyfully.

If I had rushed her, I wouldn't have heard the sweet assurances she whispered to her stuffed frog. Although she was speaking to her toy, I couldn't help but think that message was *my* message.

Once I put you in your place, you'll be fine.

When I was living distracted, I was out of place. I was discombobulated, running here and there, rushing my family and myself through life. I was missing the unforgettable Sunset Moments and the providential messages spoken in whispers.

It wasn't until my breakdown-breakthrough moment that I finally slowed down long enough to listen. That is when I felt guidance from The One who cares for me above all. It was the same message my daughter spoke today:

Once I put you in your place, you'll be fine.

I had been asking God for years what I was supposed to do with my life, but I had never slowed down long enough to listen.

Now I know.

My place is found living Hands Free.

As I let go of the rushing and stressing . . .

As I let go of the excessive to-do's and jam-packed schedules . . .

As I let go of the buzzing phone and ticking clock . . . my purpose becomes more and more clear. Make the most of each and every day. Relish the blessings in my life. Take nothing for granted.

I am simply the messenger on this life-changing journey, and it is by the grace of God and a little girl with a stuffed frog that I have this message to give: Whether we are talking about the tender words of our children or the guidance of God, we cannot hear these beautiful assurances when we are running ... running ... running.

It's time to slow down and listen. The world will undoubtedly keep whizzing by, but wait. Just wait. In times of stillness, joy and love can find you, bringing you closer to the place you are meant to be.

Not only will you be fine, but you will be super fine. And that, my friend, is a lovely way to live.

HANDS FREE WEEKLY INTENTION

Wait Joyfully

During this step on my journey I realized the high cost of my impatience. Not only did this hurried way of life create unnecessary frustration, stress, and anger, but it also robbed me of countless moments that mattered. When I felt tempted to give in to impatience, I often used one of two approaches to change my perspective:

- I asked myself, "What's the worst thing that could happen if I'm late?" This helped me acknowledge that arriving safely a few minutes late was much better than yelling at my children or getting a speeding ticket (or risking a car accident).
- I told myself that being off schedule is a blessing today—that perhaps there is an accident I am avoiding right now because I am running a little late. This helped me slow down and feel comforted in the fact that maybe a little late was exactly where I was supposed to be.

How do you feel when you are running late or have to wait? Instead of allowing frustration, anger, and stress to consume you, try Waiting Joyfully in the same manner in which you wait for a special occasion. Then sit back and watch as something beautiful unfolds and puts you in your place—the place you have always longed to be.

WHERE LIFE IS SIMPLE

I recently had the chance to reconnect with an old college friend who is now a trial attorney. Because Matt's profession brings him in contact with people and places vastly different than those in my own life, I was eager to hear about his experiences. I was especially captivated when he told me about an experience after visiting a man in a maximum-security prison.

Matt said that after leaving the prison, he felt a tangible sense of gratitude for his life. He inhaled several deep breaths of freedom, taking in a few extra doses on behalf of the incarcerated man he'd just spent the last few hours counseling.

As Matt drove away and watched the barbed-wired fortress grow small in the rearview mirror, he rolled down the window to breathe in every ounce of fresh air he could. On a whim, he decided to take the scenic route home. Easing off the gas, his decision was immediately confirmed by the untamed, natural splendor of the Kentucky mountains that enveloped him.

Eventually Matt came across a small town with a rustic country store and diner. If the ramshackle appearance of the storefront hadn't conveyed *life is simple here*, the menu choices surely would have. For lunch Matt selected the only available option, a fried bologna sandwich. As far as beverages went, there were three choices: Sprite, Coke, and water. *Oh yes, life is simple here.*

After lunch, Matt spotted a small bakery across the street and decided it was a good day for a cupcake. He figured MaMa Hazel's Bakery would be home to the best vanilla cupcake he'd ever tasted—and he'd hate to miss that.

With cupcake in hand, Matt was about to get into his vehicle when he noticed a pristine lake behind the country store. Its tranquil beauty promised sweet words of solace.

Matt contemplated for a moment about whether he should take time out of his day to sit along the water's edge, but then he spotted a large, smooth rock suitable for a perch.

At this point, something compelled me to break into Matt's reverie and say, "You make it sound like the choice was easy."

I've never forgotten Matt's response: "I had things to do, but then again, I *didn't* have things to do."

On that rock by the lake Matt had his first few moments to reflect on what had been a painful and tumultuous year. For the first time in a long time, he felt a deep sense of peace about where he was in life. He concluded by adding, "You can only enjoy life when you slow down," as if I, the Hands Free Mama, knew this already.

I did know—and how badly I wanted to make slowing down the practice of my life.

For several days I reflected on Matt's description of a simpler way. His remark about having things to do, but *not really* having things to do, refused to leave me.

I certainly wouldn't be visiting a maximum-security prison anytime soon. I knew my current responsibilities did not allow for long, leisurely drives through the mountains. And I had not endured the pain and loss Matt had experienced over the past year. Yet slowing down and basking in life's simplicities seemed like a missing element in my life. And the beauty of this missing element was that I could choose to make it happen, just as Matt did.

The following Saturday, my family had a packed schedule and several obligations. But one question kept repeating itself in my head: "Yes, we have things to do, but do we *really* have things to do?"

I felt inspired to put aside those other things and move toward what really mattered—which was to spend a simple day with my family. Scott and I had mentioned numerous times how we wanted to take our daughters fishing on a rustic lake near our home, but we never seemed to have the time. Suddenly, fishing became a priority.

We told our daughters what we were going to do; then we all excitedly donned comfortable clothes. Rather than waste precious time fixing our hair, my daughters and I simply threw on our favorite hats. Together, we packed a cooler with water and snacks. My husband grabbed the fishing poles. Within minutes we were at the lake—an expanse of liquid blue that sparkled brightly as if it had been shined and prepared just for us.

For a few bucks we rented a rusty rowboat that had a questionable-looking (but surprisingly powerful) motor. Judging by the expressions on my children's faces as the boat accelerated, one would have thought we were riding a yacht in the Caribbean.

Our biggest decisions of the day were where to anchor the boat in the vast lake and whether to use crickets or worms for bait. Once we found a perfectly shaded area, the girls cast their lines and eagerly awaited a nibble.

While we waited ...

We spotted an enormous bird and speculated about its wingspan.

We marveled at one perfect cloud.

We felt exquisite rays of sunlight streaming through the trees.

We fully reclined on the bench seat and were lulled by the calming rhythm of the water.

We gave the worms silly names and laughed until our bellies ached.

We felt deep gratitude for the beauty that surrounded us.

In other words ... we saw things we don't typically notice on a jam-packed day. We heard things we neglect to hear when we're running from one activity to the next. We felt a sense of peace and connection that just doesn't happen unless we *slow down*.

There were plenty of places we *could* have been that day. There were plenty of responsibilities, duties, and activities we *could* have accomplished. But instead we chose to go where Life Is Simple.

Now here's the best news of all, my friend. You don't have to visit a maximum-security prison to appreciate it. You don't have to drive through the mountains to see it. You don't have to stumble across an old country store to taste it.

The truth that Life Is Simple can literally be found in your backyard.

But you must *choose* it. You must choose it over the daily distractions that prevent you from hearing, seeing, and feeling what really matters.

Life Is Simple is within your reach ... if you make it a priority.

 ## HANDS FREE WEEKLY INTENTION

Go Where Life Is Simple

There were countless times during my highly distracted years when I longed to stop for picnics, take the scenic detour, and let the children dictate the pace—but I didn't. The inner drill sergeant was always spurring me on to the next thing. But as I began to free myself from daily distraction, I started wondering, *If not today, then when?* I also realized that the best moments in life almost always happen spontaneously. There doesn't have to be a master plan; there doesn't have to be a big production to have fun and make memories.

Life Is Simple can be ... creating a pile of leaves and jumping in them; making bread and sticking your hands in the gooey substance; looking up at the sky and picking a cloud to study; holding a hand and going for a walk in the sunshine. Life Is Simple can be yours if you simply slow down and choose it.

In the grand scheme of life, do you really have anything that can't wait until Monday?

Schedule unstructured family time this week.

Where is your Life Is Simple? Do you drive past it and tell yourself someday you will go there? Do you cover it up with commitments and to-do lists? Are you so far away from it that you don't even think about it anymore? Let today be different. Make Life Is Simple a priority and go there today. Experience the joy that happens only when you take time to slow down.

HANDS FREE REFLECTION

Serenity
Now Is the Time

Something happens to the concept of time in the moments following a crisis, a tragedy, or a disaster. It's as if your senses are temporarily heightened and each minute is a gift to unwrap slowly in hopes of savoring it.

That is exactly what happened in the early morning hours following the touchdown of an F2 tornado in my neighborhood. As my family braced for round two, which forecasters predicted would be even more devastating than the first, I tried to absorb every nuance, every word, and every expression.

I watched my younger daughter dress herself from start to finish,
Without rush, without haste.
I listened to my older daughter read aloud,
Without corrections or exasperated sighs.
I marveled as my children watered the potted flowers on the porch,
Without the criticisms of "too much water" or dirty hands.
I laughed as they devoured a rare treat of fluorescent-orange cheese puffs,
With no warnings of "too many" or "shirts are not napkins."
I brushed tangled hair gently and lovingly,
Without the pain that comes with a hurried pace.
I ingrained their melodic laughter to memory,
Without the thought of multitasking away their joy.
And by the grace of God, my Hands Free inner voice spoke more clearly than it ever had before.
Now is the time.
Now is the time to look into their eyes until they succumb to sleep.
Now is the time to say, "I love you," so many times you lose your voice.

Now is the time to hold them until your arms grow tired.

Now is the time to laugh until your belly hurts.

Now is the time to whisper prayers of gratitude until you account for every blessing.

Now is the time to perceive ordinary moments as gifts.

Now is the time to live in *this* moment.

Now is the time.

Now is the time.

Because you just never know what's about to come your way.

REFLECTION QUESTIONS

In what ways does your daily pace interfere with your ability to sit, relax, and be available to the ones you love?

What are some of the positive effects of taking time each day to relax or engage in a leisure activity by yourself or with a family member?

Is it difficult for loved ones to get (and maintain) your undivided attention when they talk to you? Name one practice you plan to implement that will allow you to be more available for meaningful conversations.

Chapter 6

SEE LIFE THROUGH UNDISTRACTED EYES

Clarity

Look at everything as though you were seeing it either for the first or last time. Then your time on earth will be filled with glory.

Betty Smith

LIVING DISTRACTED GAVE ME TUNNEL VISION. I was so focused on what was next—achieving my next goal, meeting my next deadline, reaching the destination—that I missed the beautiful sights and sounds along the way. Everything I did involved a master plan, and I viewed anything that threatened that plan as an annoyance or inconvenience. Not only did long lines and traffic jams cause me to become irrational, negative, and upset, but even delays caused by my own children aggravated me. My need to control every situation blinded me to the abundant gifts right under my nose. I couldn't see opportunities for meaningful connection because I was focused on the wrong things.

As I began to clear away the excess of daily distraction, the veil of negativity lifted. Taking my next step in the Hands Free journey offered me a clear view of my blessed life—even when things didn't go as planned. Suddenly, opportunities to grasp what really matters were apparent to me. Sitting at a long stoplight became a chance to pray with my eyes open. The music instructor's tardiness offered a chance for my daughter to give me a private concert. Forgetting my phone created an uninterrupted period of connection with the man I love. Through Hands Free eyes, the beauty of the world came alive, blessings were evident, and inconveniences became opportunities.

As you read through this chapter, I invite you to release the negative filter of control that obscures the everyday opportunities you have to connect, feel grateful, and enjoy life with the people you love.

BETTER THAN SLEEP

I was just drifting into peaceful slumber after a late night of writing when I heard Avery's muffled cries. I headed upstairs toward her room and met her just as she was just about to descend the first step.

Without saying a word my child held out her arms. I scooped her up, noticing immediately that she was burning with fever. I carried her back to bed, took her temperature, and gave her a few sips of cold water. Although she put up quite a fuss, I convinced her to take some fever-reducing medicine.

Finally, I tucked her into bed. I glanced at her digital clock and noted this brief encounter had only taken ten minutes. I calculated that if I raced back downstairs and fell right back to sleep, I could still get five and a half hours of sleep before morning. I'd read somewhere that people require at least five hours of slumber to avoid serious health risks later in life—and I wanted my five hours!

I hastily kissed my daughter's cheek with every intention of going straight back to bed—at least that was the plan. But I should have known that small children typically have their own plan—especially when it's midnight and they're sick.

"Would you rub my tummy, Mama?" my daughter asked in that puny, sickly voice. "Like you did when I was a baby," she added for extra leverage.

I obliged and rubbed her tummy for about thirty seconds until my hand got tired—which reminded me that my eyes were tired and my whole body was tired.

Hoping she wouldn't stir, I quietly crept out. I made a dead sprint to my bed. Ahhh ... it was just before one o'clock. Still within the five-hour range. I assured myself I could still avoid an early death.

"Mama! Mama!"

I bolted upright. And just when I thought she couldn't get any louder, the last syllable of my endearing title was accented by a blood-curdling scream.

"MaMAAAAA!"

I took two stair-steps at a time, fully expecting to see bodily fluids. But no, the only thing I saw was the pathetic expression on the face of my sick child.

"Will you rub my tummy some more?" Avery weakly asked.

This time I rubbed for two minutes. Never was I so happy to see her sucking good old Mr. Thumb. Her eyelids began to flutter, indicating she was about to succumb to sleep. With the silence and stealth of a Navy SEAL, I got up from her bed. Just as I was about to break free, her eyes flew open and questioned my hasty departure.

In a firm yet loving voice I informed her: "I'm going back to bed. You need your sleep and Mama needs her sleep. You have your ice water and your fever medicine is working now."

She obediently nodded.

Before I left, I added, "And if you need to call me, you only need to say my name once. You don't need to scream. Just say, 'Mama,' and I will come."

Again she nodded.

Just as I got back into my bed and fluffed my pillow, I heard one single, solitary, nonscreaming "Mama."

Now I was the one ready to scream.

An expletive came out of my mouth as my feet hit the floor. The clock read 1:20 a.m. I was now in the less-than-five-hours-of-sleep territory. *Just great*, I thought to myself. In one fell swoop, I had successfully elevated my risk for coronary artery disease, stroke, and hypertension!

"What is it?" I calmly asked through gritted teeth, breathing heavily from sprinting up the stairs yet again.

"Mama, I need to go to the bathroom," she whimpered.

I resisted the urge to tell her that she doesn't need me for that. Instead, I did a face-plant in her bed and mumbled, "I'll just wait here while you go."

Again, she gave me *that look*.

Once we got to the bathroom, she discovered her bag of books and her reading log waiting for her next to the toilet.

"I need to practice my reading," Avery declared.

First of all, it was now 1:30 a.m. Second, this was not a bag of books from an actual school. Oh no, this was from Big Sister's pretend school, the one where Little Sister must practice her reading—even though she doesn't really read yet. Then Mama must sign the log to indicate the student read for ten—yes, ten—whole minutes.

At this point, I could have put my foot down. I could have used my well-oiled teacher voice and declared, "Enough is enough. It's time for bed."

But for some reason, I didn't.

Maybe it was her flushed pink cheeks.

Maybe it was the way she had already opened the book and had begun to "read" by herself.

Maybe it was the way her tiny feet dangled as she sat on the potty.

Maybe it was because she desperately wanted my presence.

Maybe it was because in the midst of a trying moment, my sleep-deprived eyes were powerfully opened.

And for once, I could see what was most important in life … and it was happening right in front of my eyes. Perhaps my child's plan was far better than my own.

Avery handed me the book she had been "reading" and asked me to finish the rest. After each page, she stopped me so that she could repeat the words back as if she were actually reading. Instead of heaving a big "this will take forever" sigh, I marveled at the sight of my beautiful child.

I marveled at the tiny brown freckles on her nose.

I marveled at the remarks she interjected about her teacher reading this very book.

I marveled at the loving comments she made about her amazing sister teacher.

I marveled at the fact that even with a temperature of 101.5° and a pounding headache, this child was still smiling her sunflower-on-steroids smile.

At this point I surrendered. I no longer counted the hours left to sleep. I no longer thought about how uncomfortable it was to sit on the edge of a bathtub. I no longer thought about how fever-reducing medicine is actually a stimulant for my child (and never again to give it to her in the middle of the night).

At this point, my Hands Free perspective completely altered my view of the situation. What began as a middle-of-the-night annoyance was now an unexpected gift.

A few minutes later, Avery was settled back into bed. This time I rubbed her tummy until she fell asleep. I am not certain how long it took because I was not watching the clock. I was watching her dark eyelashes and her pajama-clad chest rise and fall. I was watching her beautiful face and the soft curls resting on her pillow.

The next morning my daughter was a bit groggy. I wondered if she even remembered the late-night ordeal.

"Can I just tell you something?" Avery asked in a scratchy voice. But she didn't wait for a response. She wrapped her arms around me and said, "You're a really great mama."

I may have missed my five-hour sleep requirement, but during the night I had gained a loyal fan—a curly-haired, perpetually smiling, number-one fan. And the lifelong health benefits of that just might make up for lost sleep.

HANDS FREE WEEKLY INTENTION

Identify Your Hands Free Enemies

The more steps I took on my journey, the more I realized this simple truth: *It is in the times I least want to be Hands Free that I most need to be Hands Free.* I began to take notice of the times when I most rebelled against being Hands Free. A major factor in my willingness to let go and live was whether or not I had enough sleep. Sleep deficiency led me to be impatient and grouchy. Being Hands Free was the last thing I wanted to be when I was in that irritable state. Once I figured this out, I immediately stopped staying up late to write or do research on the computer. I arranged my schedule so I could get at least seven or eight hours of sleep a night. Within a week, my mood improved greatly. I was more patient, loving, and calm. With a good night's sleep, being Hands Free came more naturally and more frequently.

Identify the times in your life when you most rebel against going Hands Free. Attempt to find ways you can reduce (or eliminate) the sabotaging factor(s) that get in the way of grasping what really matters.

Remember, there's more to life than the inconvenience you first see. By adjusting your perspective, there just might be an opportunity, a blessing, or a gift disguised in that "problem."

THE PAPERS TO HER HEART

My children each have a backpack they carry to and from school. Inside the backpack is a folder. Each afternoon, I empty the folders. The next day the folders come home filled to the brim.

It is just one of those things I can count on.

At the height of my overcommitted life, the mere sight of the backpacks made me queasy. I knew that the folders inside contained more papers, more responsibilities, and more activities I didn't have time to address. This feeling only added to my "cup o' stress" that was already overflowing.

As a teacher myself, I knew these communications from school were vital to the success of my children. I knew I should be thankful for every shred of information I received, every test score, every spelling test, and every chance I was given to be involved. I knew I should be grateful for the time and energy it took loving hands to evaluate these papers and place them in the folder.

But when you are overwhelmed by life, the positives get buried. When your daily planner is bursting at the seams, blessings in the ordinary, routine moments of life get covered up. All you see is *more*. More to do. More to do *right now*.

So when my children's papers came home, I felt the need to rid myself of the excess as quickly as possible. I glanced through them, ensuring there was not a permission slip or a lunch account notice, and then I pitched all of it right into the trash can.

Occasionally, I pulled out a nicely colored picture or a well-written story and offered a quick, "Great job on this, honey." Then I mailed the creation to one of the grandparents, where I knew it would be lovingly showcased on the refrigerator or windowsill.

I resorted to the grandparents because in my heart of hearts, I could not bear to throw away a potential keepsake. But in my overcommitted state, I did not have the energy to post it, place it in an album, or actually sit down and talk to my child about it.

That is how far beyond my limits my excessive array of unnecessary commitments had taken me. I was so overwhelmed by the chaos I had created that even my children's school papers were too much for me to bear.

It's hard for me to even type that sentence. When I reread it, tears come to my eyes. But if I have learned anything on this Hands Free journey, it is this: *The truth hurts, but the truth heals and brings me one step closer to the person I want to be.*

You see, each time I tossed another wad of school papers, I missed the chance to see what really mattered—and it was written in my children's very own handwriting.

But things are different now.

We now have a new end-of-the-school-day unpacking routine. After sifting through the papers in each folder, I set aside a pile of the children's work pages. Then I wait for a time when we can actually sit down and look at them together. Sometimes it isn't until bedtime and occasionally it becomes several days' worth, but I make a conscious effort to talk about these papers with my children.

We talk about the interesting word choices of Big Sister.

We talk about the fascinating color choices of Little Sister.

We talk about Big Sister's beautiful penmanship.

We talk about Little Sister's exquisite letter formation.

We talk about their growth, risk taking, creativity, and perseverance.

We talk about mistakes and how we can learn from them—and I speak from experience.

We were merely two weeks into our new routine when something remarkable began to happen. As soon as I picked up Avery from school, she talked about how she couldn't wait to show me her folder. Before we'd even made it into the house from the garage, she'd get down on her knees and begin opening her backpack. She then proceeded to show me every single item in her folder. By the look on her face, each paper was a masterpiece. Every sheet was worthy of her winning smile.

I saw a change in Natalie as well. When she came home, she quickly located her little sister's papers and called her to the sofa. Together, they went through each one.

"You sure are making the letter *D* really good!" Natalie would say to Avery, who sat there beaming.

One day during a sister-to-sister evaluation session, Avery requested I join them as quickly as possible. She pulled out a coloring booklet that was a spin-off of the children's literary classic *Brown Bear, Brown Bear, What Do You See?* With a delighted look, my child proudly announced, "I can read!" She then proceeded to read the entire booklet to Natalie and me as we both watched in amazement.

She read with inflection.

She read with pride.

She read with pure joy and delight.

And to think I used to throw away beautiful moments like these!

But things are different now.

Now I sit between my precious children peering at a pile of papers that read like a map of their day and reveal a path straight to their hearts.

From where I sit, life has never looked so good.

 ## HANDS FREE WEEKLY INTENTION

Take Ten Minutes for Show and Tell

Looking at school papers with my children has become a powerful means of connection that I hadn't expected. It takes only ten minutes, a mere fraction of the day, yet this effort allows me to know them as individuals and to know about the happenings in their lives.

I feel especially grateful for this daily ritual because it allows me into my children's world. For two long years, my distractions acted as a barrier that prevented me from really knowing my children. It is painful to think about how much of my children's world I missed as a distracted parent. Stepping into a child's world—even for a few minutes each day—is a feasible way to *know*, really know, our children. Show and Tell is a perfect way to start.

Perhaps your children want to show you something they learned or can do. Each day, offer them ten minutes of Show and Tell. The invitation to step into a child's world is open to any adult willing to put aside distraction and offer the gift of time and presence. If you have ten minutes and an open spot on the sofa, you can start right now.

IF THIS UPSETS YOU

I grabbed a box of Band-Aids, a tube of toothpaste, and a pack of gum. Because the store was bustling with shoppers that afternoon, I expected a long line at the checkout counter. Surprisingly, there was only one customer in line so I took my place a few feet behind her. As I waited, a young woman with an armful of items came and stood behind me.

Seconds later, a man with an overpowering presence strode up to the front of the store with an armful of hardware items. But rather than take his place in line, he and his multiple packs of lightbulbs planted themselves right in front of me. It would have been easy to hide every ounce of my five-foot-three-inch self beneath his looming shadow, but I decided to speak up.

"Excuse me," I said politely but firmly to the line jumper. "The end of the line is back there." I pointed to the spot behind the young woman.

In a tone reserved for hard-core criminals, the man said, "Don't you people know how to stand in line? You're supposed to get *right behind* the person in front of you! Do you need me to show you how to stand in line? Because this is *not* how you do it!"

I couldn't believe this man's outrageous tirade. I quickly surveyed the faces of the cashier and several customers to see if they were equally appalled. Clearly they were, yet nothing indicated they were going to say anything.

I simply couldn't condone this behavior, so I turned to him and said, "I don't know why you're getting so angry. It's only a line."

That is when he started spouting off about his right to be angry—but honestly, I stopped listening. There was nothing more that needed to be said. "It's only a line," pretty much summed it up. Plus, the man had gone to the back of the line just as he should have from the beginning.

As Mr. Line Crasher stood there continuing his rant, I said a prayer of gratitude.

It wasn't that long ago that I too would have become agitated if

I'd had to stand in line at the post office or grocery store. It wasn't long ago that I huffed and puffed when I couldn't find matching socks or if the dishwasher wouldn't close properly. It wasn't long ago that little things set me off, like an out-of-order gas pump with no signage or an unexpected detour on my usual course of travel.

Although I never had a meltdown like the man at the drugstore, it was not unusual for me to act like such minor inconveniences were going to ruin my day—and sometimes I actually let them.

But things are different now.

As I take more steps on my journey to let go of distraction and grasp what really matters, I gain a new perspective. And this is what I have found:

When I'm not rushing through life at high speed,

When my schedule isn't jam-packed with every spare moment accounted for,

When my attention isn't consumed by the buzzing electronic device gripped tightly in my hand,

When I'm freed from unnecessary pressures,

Then minor inconveniences like waiting in line don't bother me so much. I actually start to see *all* moments—even the bad, frustrating, and tiresome ones—as gifts.

Why?

Because I am alive to experience them . . . and the significance of that fact should not be underestimated.

I've discovered that seeing the not-so-great moments as gifts makes the good ones even more breathtakingly beautiful. In fact, I have a special name for those moments. They are Moments That Matter. I started a list of them not too long ago. I won't bore you with the whole list, but here are a few:

RACHEL'S MOMENTS THAT MATTER

- Seeing the joyful expression on Avery's face when she demonstrates her newfound ability to read
- Standing beside Natalie as she confidently speaks to our congregation about sponsoring Priscilla through Compassion International

- Watching Scott lovingly teach our daughters how to throw a football
- Acknowledging the miraculous fact that both my parents are alive to know and bond with my children
- Pausing to spot a beautiful cloud formation that looks like a cross in the sky
- Spending time laughing and talking with a friend who allows me to be myself

On the same day as the incident at the store, I received a message from a blog reader—a providential sign along my Hands Free journey that indicated I'm headed in the right direction. Every single thing I believed about the line crasher's overreaction was confirmed in this powerful note.

> When our daughter Lexi was nine months old, we were back in the hospital again. She had just had some tests and was back in her room recovering. One of the heart surgeon's nurses came to check on her. As she was covering up my sleeping baby after examining her, she said, "Enjoy her while you have her."
>
> This nurse knew something I didn't. Most people would have been upset by her words, and not that I wasn't, but you have no idea how glad I was to know that she was being honest. And I chose to listen.
>
> From that point on, I took it all in—all the moments of love and joy, despair and frustration, the hard times and the good times. We got almost fourteen years of moments with our Lexi. But most of all, I spent those moments letting her know she was loved.

I conclude this story with a question I ask myself when I start to become agitated about a defective gas pump, slow Internet service, or an overcooked steak:

If you get upset about the little things in life, how in the world will you handle the big things?

Instead of seething over the little things, let's focus on the Moments That Matter and collect them—collect them while we can. We never know when one of life's big things will arrive without warning and make us long for the time when standing in line was the biggest problem of our day.

HANDS FREE WEEKLY INTENTION

Create a Moments That Matter List

My life took a positive turn when I stopped allowing minor inconveniences to upset me. Once I surrendered control, trusting that God had a plan for my day and my life, I began to notice countless opportunities to collect the Moments That Matter. Here are a few examples:

- Waiting for the doctor became an opportunity to really talk to my child.
- Being served by a poorly skilled waiter became a life lesson in compassion for my children.
- Getting caught in a rainstorm on the day of the swim meet became a chance to share an umbrella and jump in puddles.
- Having a delayed flight became the chance to thank a military service member who was also on my flight.

Whenever I found myself getting upset over life's little annoyances, I thought about those who are truly suffering, those who could only wish their problems were as insignificant as mine. Offering myself this awareness quickly put my minor problems into perspective.

Purchase a small notebook and start a Moments That Matter list or journal. Keep the notebook handy in your purse or briefcase or on your bedside table so you can jot down the meaningful experiences that occur each day. By making Hands Free the practice of your life, you have undoubtedly already gained uncountable moments that would have been missed had you continued to live a distracted life. Well, those moments can be multiplied when your perspective on life aligns with your Hands Free actions. By keeping an ongoing list of Moments That Matter, you will be more apt to notice the positives in your life. This newfound awareness will inspire a perpetual feeling of gratitude, which fuels a Hands Free life. Let go of the need to control the outcome. Let go of the need for situations to go exactly as planned. Let go and open your eyes for a clear view to a fulfilling life.

HANDS FREE REFLECTION

Clarity
Notice the Good

To see the high marks on the report card before I see the low ones ...
To see her beautiful swimming form before
I notice what place she comes in ...
To see she's dressed herself before I notice the winter
boots and tank top combination ...
To see she's made her own breakfast before I notice the
cereal scattered across the counter ...
To see the artistic flair in her creation before I notice the mess ...
To see her love for music before I notice the out-of-tune notes ...
To see the effort and the attempt before I see
the mistakes and the shortcomings ...
To see the beauty and goodness before I see
the flaws and imperfections ...
To see the opportunities before I notice the inconveniences ...
To see the promises of each day before I notice the challenges ...
This is how I want to live.
To notice the good—always the good—before anything
else ... and above all else.

REFLECTION QUESTIONS

"It is in the times I least want to be Hands Free that I most *need* to be Hands Free." What does that statement mean to you?

Are there tasks within your children's daily routine (such as bedtime, homework, meal preparation, or car pool) that you currently view as an inconvenience that might actually be an opportunity to connect? How might you change your perspective to see the hidden gifts in the midst of monotony or trying times?

When you find yourself becoming agitated over minor inconveniences or trivial annoyances, what might you think about or say to yourself to keep things in proper perspective?

Chapter 7

SAY YES TO WHAT MATTERS

Simplification

You can do anything, but not everything.
David Allen

BY THE TIME I REACHED THIS POINT IN MY JOURNEY, I had a good handle on my electronic device usage and my pace of life had slowed considerably. But another distraction, or perhaps I should say a hundred *little* distractions, still consumed my time, focus, and energy. My inclination to say yes to any and all requests created an unending cycle of busyness that sabotaged my relationships, health, and happiness. My God-given talents were spread so thinly they felt like burdens instead of gifts. The light in my eyes that once came from serving others had all but diminished. I was so concerned with pleasing others that I lost sight of my own passions. It was time to face reality. I would never be truly Hands Free until I released myself from the weight of an overcommitted life.

This next step was the key to freeing myself permanently from an overscheduled existence. Through extensive soul-searching and divine guidance, I learned how to be selective. By eliminating unnecessary commitments, I was able to invest my time, attention, and talents in what truly mattered to me. For the first time in my life, my energies were given strictly to activities that aligned with my life's purpose.

Protecting your time and talents from activities that leave you depleted is an essential step in establishing a sustainable Hands Free life. As you read the three stories that follow, I invite you to consider the cost of an overcommitted life. Through this important step in the journey, I hope you will be inspired to abandon the do-it-all mentality and pinpoint the commitments and activities that really matter to you. Rather than spending time on extraneous duties that exhaust and burden, you can learn how to save your most valuable resources for the people and activities that bring you true joy and fulfillment.

MISSING MORE THAN LIFE

I can still see her standing proudly on stage in her pint-sized cap and gown, singing songs about growing up and going to kindergarten. I will admit: I cried. But there was something more—something painful that I had never allowed myself to fully acknowledge until the moment I saw Avery on the day of her preschool graduation.

As my child stood there, beaming her beautiful smile, waving and looking directly into my eyes, I felt the urge to fall to my knees. I was so grateful I wasn't sitting at her high school graduation looking at a child I did not know. I could have easily cruised through eighteen years of her life blindly unaware of everything I was missing. I had come frighteningly close to missing it all.

You see, I lost two years with my daughter. It was not because of a personal tragedy, an illness, or because I was incapacitated. No, tragically my two-year absence was of my own doing. This is not one of my shining moments as a parent, but I share it in the hope that one person will read this and say, "That is me. I'm on the verge of losing something sacred I'll never get back."

When Avery was two, Natalie went to kindergarten. I spent the previous five years as a stay-at-home mom, moving to several new cities in a short time period, focusing solely on my family. So when Natalie went to kindergarten and Avery was no longer a baby, I dove into volunteer activities that stimulated my mind, allowed me to use my God-given talents, and engaged me in conversations with other adults—activities I had been desperately missing. With each successful event I chaired, I felt validated. I discovered an identity other than "Mom." I was filling a five-year void.

But I took it too far.

While I was doing good for so many, my family got lost, particularly my two-year-old daughter with strawberry-blonde hair and a freckle-kissed nose. Because of her contented nature, she allowed me to shuffle her around from one meeting to another. She patiently tolerated my unending volunteer duties and ever-willingness to assist in school, church, and community events whenever help was requested. My child never once complained about the completely stressed-out and overtaxed woman she called "Mama." My sweet two-year-old just went right along with my overscheduled life, not knowing she was being given the leftovers, the worthless scraps of time and attention from her stretched-too-thin mother.

I had a nagging feeling about my excessive number of commitments, but I justified my bursting-at-the-seams calendar by arguing that my involvement was needed. I effectively denied the fact that these activities were sabotaging my relationships, my health, and my happiness.

But that denial ended on the day of my pivotal breakdown-breakthrough moment. I had to stop in the middle of a morning run because I was unable to see the road in front of me. As a thousand tears flooded my eyes, one for every precious moment I had missed, I realized I didn't want to live this way—not one more day. But how? How could I stop being the person everyone expected me to be?

In that moment I felt as if God had placed his hand on my head—like a parent would do to a child—and said, "If you allow yourself to rest, I will renew you and fill you with peace." It suddenly occurred to me that perhaps "doing" for God was not the way he intended for me to live. Instead, perhaps I should try "being" for God. This revelation gave me permission to incorporate moments of rest—simply *being* for God and *being* for my family. I vowed to stop exerting my efforts in a hundred directions and place my trust in *one* direction.

That very day I made my first attempt at just *being*. I started with Avery, who I felt was the greatest victim of my admired ability to "do it all." I simply sat beside her—listening, watching, and absorbing every miraculous tidbit she offered me. Instantly, I was filled with a peace and a sense of connection that was foreign to my overscheduled existence. I continued these moments of simply being, and through them, I got to know my daughter.

I know . . .

She is ticklish right under her chin, in that tender spot beneath her little round face that still holds a soft layer of cushion.

Her upper left tooth is a little crooked from sucking her thumb since she was two weeks old.

When she laughs too hard she gets the hiccups, which makes her laugh even harder.

I know . . .

She gets this dreamy look on her angelic face when she hears stories about herself as a baby.

She says "meed" instead of "need," and I can't bear the thought that someday soon she will pronounce it correctly.

She refers to dandelions as "wishing flowers" and makes the exact same wish every time she blows on one: "I hope I can live in Disney World."

I know . . .

She generously offers to help me make muffins and cookies and then magically disappears after she licks the beater.

She can't quite get the two-finger F chord on her tiny ukulele but the C chord sounds like pure heaven.

She listens intently to songs on the radio and looks disappointed when she has to refute the lyrics of a song, "That singer is wrong, Mama. It's never too late to apologize."

I know . . .

She is an excellent salad maker, except for the fact that she eats all the red peppers before they make it into the bowl.

She forms her hands into little balls when she runs.

She gets overly excited when pouring her own milk into a glass.

I know . . .

She loves to entertain a crowd . . . the bigger the better.

She voluntarily asks to take a nap when she is tired.

She loves the distinct flavors found in hummus and sushi rolls but claims toothpaste is "too spicy."

And I know . . .

She somehow smells like gumdrops when she first wakes up (even though she refused to use the spicy toothpaste).

She sings made-up songs and somehow makes them sound like the most beautiful melodies.

She can actually make my heart stop when she wraps her arms around my neck and whispers, "You're my best friend, Mama."

This list contains a mere fraction of what I have come to know about my younger daughter since I stopped doing so much outside the sacred perimeters of God and family. I look forward to knowing my daughter better each day through periods of simply being, listening, and observing. And what a joyful moment it will be when my radiant, eighteen-year-old daughter stands proudly at her high school graduation. I will be able to say, "That's my daughter, Avery. I know her. I know every good and precious and miraculous thing about her."

I will be forever grateful for the unforgettable lesson I received before it was too late—the one that I repeat in my head each day to remind myself how I want to live:

Do less—you're missing more than life.

Be more—you've got so much to live for.

 ## HANDS FREE WEEKLY INTENTION

Envision Future Relationships

A vital component to creating a sustainable Hands Free life was setting aside ten minutes each day for personal reflection. During this uninterrupted quiet time, I read a daily devotional or prayed. It was in those quiet moments that I experienced divine whispers about how I should spend my time. I began to see the big picture—a glimpse of what I hoped my future relationship with my children would look like. But to get a handle on my overscheduled life, I had to face some difficult truths. I realized that if I continued to invest the bulk of my time and attention outside of my family, my grown children would be strangers to me. But if I replaced hours of *doing* with moments of **being**, my children's recollection of their childhood might be something like this:

The way my mom treated me let me know I was a priority in her life. She looked at me when we talked. She was never too busy to listen to what I had to say. I turned to her when I had a problem or when I had good news to share. I loved to tell my mom things because she really listened— listened with her eyes, heart, and soul. And now she is still the person I want to talk to when I have something to ask or share.

This week, set aside ten to fifteen minutes a day for prayerful reflection. Consider the pace of your life and where you are investing your limited time and energies. If you find it helpful, use a notepad or journal to reflect on questions like these:

- Does the amount of time and attention I currently offer to my child convey that he or she is a top priority in my life? Where do I invest the bulk of my time and energies? Are these activities fulfilling to me?
- Does my current schedule allow for time spent simply being with my child? Do I have any extracurricular commitments or time-wasting distractions that I could eliminate in order to spend a few minutes of special time each day with my child?

LOVE ALL I DO

When the caller said she heard I was great at organizing large groups and making things happen, I knew what was coming next. *Would you be willing to head up a really worthy project that does so much good for so many kids in the community?*

My mouth opened, and I felt like there was only one right answer—the one that would make her happy. And I knew that what I wanted to say felt like the wrong answer.

Declining these kinds of requests has always been difficult, if not impossible, for me. As a lifelong sufferer of what I call the Three P Syndrome (Perfectionistic People Pleaser), I know the right answer—the one people expect to hear—is *yes*.

So I lived half of my adult life doing everything I was asked to do, and doing it at the highest level of quality and effort—even if it killed me. In fact, I did everything so well that nearly every single day another volunteer request magically came my way.

But you know how that story ends. My servant heart and lack of boundaries were a near-lethal combination. So I learned to say no. Still, on occasion, it's hard to say, like when one perfectly nice woman was on the other end on the phone waiting to hear me say, "Sure, I'll do it."

But this time I said, "I'm sorry, but I won't be able to do that this year."

And then I waited.

Miraculously, the lights did not flicker, my hair did not fall out, and the world did not come to a screeching halt.

The woman simply said, "Thank you." And that was that!

Although it felt awkward, *no* was the right answer—for me … and for my family … and for our life at this juncture. My heart leapt with joy.

So how did I finally get to the place where the word *no* did not leave me a guilt-ridden mess, wondering if I could somehow help out more if I just stopped sleeping altogether?

Let's just say, it didn't happen overnight.

When I experienced my breakdown-breakthrough moment, I realized I had to be intentional about how I spend my precious time here on earth. David Allen's quote, "You can do anything, but you can't do everything," spoke volumes to me. I made a mission statement consisting of what I most wanted to accomplish in life. I called it my "Life List," and it was surprisingly short.

RACHEL'S LIFE LIST

- I want to know who my children and spouse are as individuals by being a constant presence and source of love and support in their lives.
- I want to use my God-given gifts as teacher, writer, and encourager to write and speak words that help people grasp what really matters in life.

I began using my Life List whenever I was asked to assist in any activity outside of my regular responsibilities. If the request did not align with the goals on my list, I said no. It took time, but eventually my extracurricular commitments were scaled down to one or two yearly projects that I was passionate about and directly involved my family. Had I not created a Life List, I would not be where I am today. You would not be holding this book. There would be no Hands Free Mama. My children would have significantly fewer memories of their mom being happy, silly, spontaneous, interactive, grateful, and fully present. I would have continued to miss more Sunset Moments than I could count.

Now here's the funny part.

Every day I get out the daily planner I bought before becoming Hands Free. I no longer use it to document appointments and important dates, but I do use it to maintain a regular writing schedule and plan blog posts. But what I find so humorous about my planner is the slogan written boldly on the front: "Do It All."

A *Do It All Calendar* for the Hands Free Mama.

Maybe it's just me, but I think that's funny.

Do It All Rachel is so yesterday.

I've thought about covering up the slogan because every time I see the words *Do It All*, I feel queasy. What is it about that phrase that bothers me so much?

There's certainly nothing wrong with the *do* part of the equation. We all need to *do* things to feel productive, purposeful, validated, and alive.

And I don't think there's anything wrong with the *all* part. To me, *all* conveys diving into something with your whole heart, your passion, and your energy.

So it comes down to the word *it*. That little pronoun is the troublemaker.

It means settling for whatever comes your way. *It* means doing something simply because you are asked to. *It* means saying yes through gritted teeth because you just can't say no. *It* means not being intentional and selective about how you use your precious time on this earth.

So if there's nothing wrong with the *do* and nothing wrong with the *all*, what *would* be a better slogan on a daily calendar for the Hands Free life?

Love All I Do.

Doesn't that sound appealing? Doesn't it sound liberating? Doesn't it sound well … doable?

When it comes down to the extracurricular obligations in my life, I chose to *Love All I Do* rather than *Do It All*. And when I think about the small list of duties I've agreed to participate in this year at my children's school, our church, and in our community, I see a theme. I see a list comprised of my true passions—opportunities to help while fulfilling my life's purpose.

But wait. It gets even better.

Because the commitments on that list do not fill 365 spaces in my calendar, there is breathing room. There is room for laughing, playing, memory making, and (gasp) maybe even a little relaxing with the people I love the most. There is room for what really matters. There is room to *live*.

I think it's time to change the slogan on my Hands Free daily planner.

Love All I Do Rachel is very *now* … and she is here to stay.

 ## HANDS FREE WEEKLY INTENTION

Create Your Own Life List

Several years ago, I read the following passage in Patti Digh's brilliant book *Life Is a Verb*:

> Early in her career [Toni] Morrison worked at Random House
> publishers. One day her head exploded just as mine had, and
> she started her list of to-do items. She wrote pages and pages
> of things that she must do. Faced with the long list, she sat and
> looked at it for a long while, finally asking herself one question:
> What is it I must do or I shall die?
>
> After answering that question, there were only two things left
> on her to-do list: 1) Be a mother to her children. 2) Write.*

Digh's words aroused an awakening in me. I realized that *I* controlled what my daily to-do list looked like. And those day-to-day lists would eventually make up how I spent my life. By continuing to omit my family and dream of becoming an author from the priority list, I would never fulfill my God-given purpose.

Once I began my Hands Free journey, Patti Digh's words came back to me time and time again. On the day I burned my to-do list, I did exactly what my heart desired—I spent time with my family and wrote. It was one of the happiest days of my life.

What is truly important to you? Spending time with your family? Volunteering for a certain organization? Being fit and healthy? Deepening your prayer life? Once you identify what really matters to you, get out your calendar and compare your extracurricular commitments to your Life List. If an activity doesn't support an item on that list, begin making plans to eliminate it from your schedule.

You have the power to control how you spend your time. You have the power to control how you use your gifts and talents. Because once you've spent all your time and used all your talents, there are no leftovers to give yourself and your family. Believe me, I tried that for two long years. It almost cost me what is most precious.

*Patti Digh, *Life Is a Verb: 37 Ways to Wake Up, Be Mindful, and Live Intentionally* (Guilford, Conn.: skirt! books, 2008), 186–87.

CLOSER THAN I WAS BEFORE

Despite my Hands Free mission,

Despite my intention to let go and live,

Despite having a Life List,

I still have days when I feel completely overwhelmed.

As in the case on this particular Monday.

Like an incompetent skater on very thin ice, if one more thing was added to my already full routine, I was going to plummet into a dismal abyss.

Although I had drastically scaled down my once-overflowing commitment list, the things I was still committed to always seemed to converge on the same day—which happened to be the same the day the stomach bug hit my house … which happened to be the same day I grocery shopped without my wallet … which happened to be the same day the toilet overflowed.

Add those extra little mishaps to a person's daily responsibilities, and I'll give you one completely stressed out, highly irritable maniac.

That was me on this particular Monday.

I was as far from being Hands Free as I ever wanted to be, and I hated it. I felt like my head was about to explode. I felt like my blood pressure rivaled the high readings of my preeclampsia days. I felt like I couldn't get enough done in the waking hours, so I used sleeping hours. I couldn't do the things I wanted to do, like play with my kids and write my stories. Hands Free Rachel was thrown under a bus. Ultra-organized, hyperproductive, control-freak drill sergeant Rachel was running the show.

Did I mention I hated it?

And then came this question over and over: *Why did you do this to yourself? How did you allow this to happen when you are supposed to be living Hands Free?*

I didn't have an answer. And I still don't have one. In fact, I realize I may never have the answer. Perhaps this is how life will go ... five Hands Free baby steps forward and one giant Non–Hands Free step back.

Yet even as I was giving myself a major lecture about the perils of overcommitment, my Hands Free inner voice came to the rescue. It lovingly reminded me that at least now I am aware. There was a time not too long ago when this completely stressed-out feeling was the norm. My inner drill sergeant never took a rest. Every day was like this particular Monday, devoid of what really matters and unaware of what was really important. Life was all about marking things off the list and looking ahead to what was next.

In this moment of recognition and awareness, I saw what I *didn't* want my life to look like. In fact, the Non–Hands Free version of myself made me so sad that I wanted to look away.

The truth hurts, but the truth heals — and allows change to occur.

I realized with clarity that ...

I don't want too many things on my plate anymore.

I don't want to rush my daughters through life so I can make it to a meeting on time.

I don't want my family to take last place on the priority list.

I don't want the compulsion to check my phone or email to grip me like an addiction I cannot control.

By getting a bitter taste of my Pre–Hands Free life, my commitment to continue my journey was powerfully renewed. I may not have the answer, but through the experience of a bad Monday, I gleaned these priceless facts:

I am farthest from the answer when ...

- I feel like I am perpetually late.
- There is not enough time to get proper sleep or exercise.
- I quickly inhale my meals standing at the kitchen counter.

- I don't have time to have meaningful conversations with the people I love.
- I don't look into my children's eyes when they speak to me.
- I feel angry and negative for no reason.
- I yell at my children when I am really yelling at myself for creating the chaos I am in.
- I don't have time to write or dream.
- My thoughts are interrupted by the distraction of the phone and email.
- I hold myself to an unrealistic standard of perfection.
- My inner critic is cruel and unloving.

I am closest to the answer when ...

- I am lying beside one of my daughters talking about life before bedtime.
- I am running along a deserted road to the tunes of my favorite songs and warm sunshine on my face.
- I am chronicling my thoughts and my dreams with a pencil and a notebook.
- I am sharing the joys and struggles of my life with my spouse, parents, and dearest friends.
- I have quiet, reflective moments of gratitude and prayer.
- My phone and computer are turned off.
- I am doing something for someone who can never repay me.
- The boxes in my calendar contain healthy white space.
- I am accepting and loving toward myself, despite my imperfections and insecurities.
- I give my body the nutritious food that it craves and the sleep that it needs.

As this particular Monday came to a close, I had trouble sleeping. In fact, soon after I fell asleep I awoke feeling as if I'd just received a long-awaited revelation. I stumbled out to the kitchen looking for something to write on. At the beginning of my journey, it was an envelope from the zoo that I used to record my

"What I Would've Missed" revelation; this time it was my child's progress report. In my mind was the answer to a problem that had caused years of angst and turmoil; I couldn't afford to let my impending sleep erase this life-changing epiphany. This is what I scribbled on the back on my child's progress report that I will undoubtedly keep forever:

> *Just listen to your heart—it will not mislead you.*
> *Just let things happen—the most meaningful moments arise unplanned.*
> *Stop trying to control. Just let things be.*
> *Just let things be—so you can live.*

I don't know the answer. But I'm certain I'm getting closer. Yes, I am getting closer to what really matters. And I think *closer* on the Hands Free journey is a very good place to be.

 ## HANDS FREE WEEKLY INTENTION

Pinpoint Your Closest and Farthest Moments

We all have good days and bad days. We know there are times when we are more present and more focused on what's important than we are at other times. So the key is to figure out when those times are. Instead of discouraging me, pinpointing the times in my life when I felt most Non–Hands Free actually empowered me. I remember standing at the kitchen counter eating my lunch one day when it hit me that I had also eaten breakfast there too. A huge red flag went up in my mind. I knew that eating while standing up was an unhealthy practice, preventing me from enjoying my food, making conversation, and expressing gratitude for my meal. I took a look at that day's events and attempted to figure out what I could do differently the next day to prevent this from happening again. The next day, I ate all three meals at the table. Being mindful of my Closest and Farthest Moments enabled me to get myself back on track despite setbacks along my journey.

Right now—right here in this book if you have to—jot down your Closest and Farthest Moments. What stands out to you most about your lists? Make every effort to be in one of the Closest Moments today. And the next time you find yourself in a Farthest Moment, give yourself grace and simply ask yourself what you can do differently next time.

 *HANDS FREE REFLECTION*

Simplification
Kid World

As we get farther and farther away from childhood, the demands and stresses of life increase. We tend to forget that we have the power to say yes to the delights of our heart and soul. But to do so, we must abandon the pressure to do-it-all; we must surrender the need to please everyone; we must protect our time and energies from that which depletes and exhausts.

Whenever I need to be reminded of the simple joys I want in my life, I step into Kid World. It is in the presence of children that I remember exactly how I want to live out my precious days on earth.

In Kid World . . .
There is time.
Time to stop and admire mystic clouds and find the beauty in a
    dandelion.
Time to give your waitress a hug.
Time to do it yourself . . . even if it takes longer . . . even if it's not
    perfect.

In Kid World . . .
There is confidence.

Confidence to celebrate bathing-suit season.

Confidence to pair unusual style combinations and wear them in
  public.

Confidence to dance when everyone is watching.

In Kid World . . .

There is safety.

Safety in the glow of a bedroom nightlight.

Safety in Daddy's arms.

Safety in homemade forts built with your sister as rain beats against
  the windowpane.

In Kid World . . .

There is beauty.

Beauty in freckle-kissed noses and grass-stained feet.

Beauty in mispronounced words like "liberry" and "funder storm."

Beauty in open-mouthed laughter and disobedient curls on a warm
  summer night.

In Kid World . . .

There is comfort.

Comfort in the smell of Mom's hair.

Comfort in that certain pair of pajamas despite being two sizes too
  small.

Comfort in worn teddy bears that sleep under your breath.

In Kid World . . .

The gaps between the teeth are wide.

Individual differences are noticed, but openly accepted.

Laughter between friends cures all ills.

Apple seeds can become trees if planted with love.

In Kid World . . .

Forgiveness is abundant.

Flaws are easily overlooked.

Bad breath and crazy hair are signs of good sleep.
There's no such thing as too many stuffed animals.

In Kid World . . .
There is no need to hurry.
Hope is never lost.
Love is an endless commodity.
And the world looks beautiful from down here.

REFLECTION QUESTIONS

Is the number of extracurricular commitments in your life a point of contention with a loved one or your own inner voice? Do you feel the concern is justified? Why or why not?

Do you say yes to extracurricular requests and then resent the time you spend doing them? What response could you prepare to say the next time you are asked to do something that does not align with your Life List?

Chapter 8

SILENCE THE INNER CRITIC

Acceptance

Every second that you spend on doubting your worth, every moment that you use to criticize yourself; is a second of your life wasted, is a moment of your life thrown away. It's not like you have forever, so don't waste any of your seconds, don't throw even one of your moments away.

C. JoyBell C.

I BEGAN MY HANDS FREE JOURNEY to curb the electronic distractions that sabotaged my relationships and my moments that mattered. But as I quieted down the *external* sources of distraction in my life, I discovered that *internal* distractions were just as damaging as a buzzing phone and an overscheduled agenda. Messages of shame, inadequacy, fear, doubt, and criticism popped into my head like undeletable email messages in an inbox. These debilitating comments paralyzed me. They prevented me from enjoying life, taking risks, forming deep relationships, and revealing my true self. By this point in my journey, I had squelched the incessant beeps of external distraction. Now I knew it was time to silence my inner critic so I could stop hiding behind a façade and start living a more authentic life.

This step in the journey helped me to abandon the unachievable pursuit of perfection. At this juncture, I was determined to stop comparing myself to photoshopped images of celebrities and supermodels, and I yearned to reject cultural standards of beauty and success. My harsh inner critic was gradually replaced by a kind, loving, and accepting voice. I called this encouraging dialogue my "victory song of self-acceptance." By exchanging my negative inner critic for positive self-talk, I began to believe I was enough. No longer did I decline social invitations if my pants felt a little snug that day. No longer did my children have to look perfect each time we stepped out of the house. No longer did I have to hide my flaws and keep up an exhausting façade. For the first time in my life, I saw myself as a beautifully imperfect human being who makes mistakes and learns from them. Best of all, I saw the changes I was making reflected in my children's eyes. My new self-acceptance enveloped them like a blanket of worthiness. Through this monumental step in my journey, I was spared from years of torment and missed opportunities—and my children were too.

The stories in this chapter illustrate how negative self-talk can sabotage your Moments That Matter, threaten your happiness, and damage your sense of self-worth. I invite you to release your critical inner dialogue so your hands are free to embrace your own "victory song of self-acceptance." By silencing your inner critic, the opportunity to embark on an imperfectly beautiful life comes within reach.

MAY I OFFER YOU MY HAT?

The hardest days for me to grasp what really matters are my "some days." What do I mean by "some days"? These days are not pretty, but they are real. Here are my "some days":

Some days, I feel lost in a sea of *worthless*, *uncertain*, *ugly*, and *damaged*.

Some days, I measure my worth by things that will mean nothing in the end.

Some days, I question my abilities, my purpose, and my relevance.

Some days, I hunger for freedom, silence, and solitude.

Some days, I just want to give up.

Some days, I just want to go away.

Some days, there are no pretty words in my heart.

Some days, there are no pretty words in my head.

Some days, there are no pretty words for the woman in the mirror staring back at me, who wonders if she'll ever measure up.

Those are my "some days," but then there are the "hat days." Thank goodness for the hat days.

You see, around the time I started my Hands Free journey, I began wearing hats. Stylish, yes ... sporty, yes ... but that is not why I wore them. Rather than spending time washing and styling my hair, I began throwing on a hat so I could use that precious time to have fun with my family. Throwing on a hat was not a conscious decision at the time. In fact, I didn't even notice that my hat collection was growing and that I was wearing them several times a week.

But someone else did.

And the fact that this particular person noticed reveals one of the greatest unexpected gifts of living Hands Free. The fact that this particular person noticed my hats provides me with daily ammunition to battle the negative voice that permeates my "some days." And I am finally starting to believe that I can win this battle.

This is my story ...

During a lesson in Avery's class, the children were asked, "What do you want to be when you grow up?" Based on their answers, the students created a paper-doll model of themselves as grown-ups. Among the classroom paper-doll collection of doctors, teachers, firefighters, dolphin trainers, and veterinarians, there was a woman in a pink outfit wearing a brightly colored bike helmet of some sort. That doll belonged to my child. Her teacher was kind enough to hand-deliver the creation to me and provide an explanation.

"This is what Avery wants to be when she grows up," her teacher explained as she held up the lovingly decorated doll. She pointed directly to the hat and said, "Avery wants to be a mom, but not just any mom. She wants to be a mom who wears a hat—a mom just like you." If that weren't enough to make me crumple into an emotional mess, her teacher added, "Your daughter has the biggest heart."

Later that evening, I proudly held up my child's artwork for my husband and recited exactly what her teacher told me. Without missing a beat my husband said, "A hat? The biggest heart? That's you. That is *all* you."

In that moment, my child's paper doll was a healing salve on my too-often-beaten-down spirit. What Avery thought of me was the opposite of what my inner critic had been telling me all these years. It suddenly dawned on me that the cruel self-talk I allowed on my "some days" caused tunnel vision that went straight to my flaws—imperfections no else seemed to notice and perhaps existed only in my head. My inner critic had encouraged unrealistic standards that were often inaccurate, not to mention shallow, measurements of my worth.

With tape in hand, I went straight to my bathroom mirror and taped my child's paper doll front and center. Each day, it gave me a more realistic and loving standard of measurement for my authentic Hands Free life.

As I stood before the mirror, I made a vow ...

I vow to stop measuring my worth by the circumference of my waist, the cleanliness of my house, or the state of my children's hair when they walk out the door.

I vow to stop measuring myself by how fast I can run a mile, the marks on my child's report card, and how many academic degrees hang on my wall.

I vow to stop measuring myself by the number of bulges, sags, wrinkles, and scars on my body.

Because in reality, these things don't matter. The only thing that really matters is this: I am a loving mother to my children, and I am raising them to be kind and loving people.

And that is enough. In fact, it's everything.

I vow to start seeing the same woman my daughter sees when she looks at me—the woman she wants to be when she grows up, and the woman she is already starting to become. I choose to start seeing the woman who wears hats rather than washing and styling her hair because time doesn't wait for perfect hair ... and time won't wait while I get all my imperfections sorted out ... and time won't wait while I try to become more like that woman on the cover of the magazine ... and time surely won't wait while I foolishly try to "do it all."

Time does not wait. Therefore, I chose to stop wasting time.

I chose to stop looking at the things I am not and start looking at all the things I am.

And I happen to think I look pretty darn good in a hat.

HANDS FREE WEEKLY INTENTION

Make It a Hat Day

My Hands Free journey took me to an unexpected place. Instead of skimming the surface, I went deep—and that takes more courage than simply glossing over the rough parts. By taking that difficult look inward, I freed myself. No longer was I held captive in that dark and lonely place of cruel comparison and harsh judgment. No longer did I concern myself with what other people thought of the way I looked or the choices I made for my family. Through the loving light of authenticity, I saw the same beautiful woman my daughter saw—the woman with a big heart who often chose to throw on a hat rather than style her hair. My hats represented my surrender from the pursuit of perfection. They offered a chance to let go, laugh, be silly, and have fun. Each time I put one on, I was in the frame of mind to be Hands Free.

Make it a Hat Day. Choose one day this week to literally or figuratively throw on a hat ... any hat will do. Do not look in the mirror; do not worry about your appearance. Now do something you might never otherwise have time to do. Be with the people you rarely have enough time to see. By spending less time worrying about the things that don't matter, you will have more time for the things that do matter!

YOU ARE BEAUTIFUL

The other day I stopped at the drugstore for a few items. It was an extremely hot day, and I had just finished working out. I would have preferred to shower before the quick shopping trip, but sunscreen, Band-Aids, and an anniversary card for my parents couldn't wait.

I was comparing the outrageous price of spray sunscreen versus lotion sunscreen when a male voice startled me out of my SPF price-comparing reverie. "I just gotta say, you are beautiful," the man stated as casually as he would tell me my shoe was untied or that Banana Boat lasts longer than Coppertone. But he didn't say those things. He said, "You are beautiful." And then the young man, who appeared to be half my almost forty years, added, "Go Tarheels."

I looked down at my fossilized college T-shirt just to be sure he was talking to me. The UNC emblem was barely visible, so I was still not convinced I was the recipient of his unexpected compliment. I looked over my shoulder to make sure a Scarlett Johansson look-alike wasn't behind me, coyly deciding which tanning oil would produce the best results. With no other human being in sight, I accepted the fact that he was indeed talking to me, but he must have had very bad eyesight.

In my hand, I gripped a tube of sunscreen I would have paid fifty bucks for just to vaporize myself out of the store. As embarrassment climbed my neck in a prominent red hue, I sprinted to the checkout counter. Who needs Band-Aids and store-bought cards anyway? I decided masking tape would work perfectly as Band-Aids and Hallmark cards are completely overrated anyway. I was certain my parents would love a homemade anniversary card this year.

I am not even sure I waited for my change from the cashier. I scurried to my vehicle, slamming the door with vigor. Once I was in the safety of my car, I had a moment to reflect. I tilted the rearview mirror down until I could see my reflection, but then I quickly tilted it back up. I surely did not see anything qualifying as beautiful there.

In that moment of bewilderment and shock, the words of a dear friend came back to me. She had recently posted an array of vacation pictures on Facebook. A particular photo of her in the album captivated me. It was a close-up of her face. She wore not a stitch of make-up, and she was laughing. In the comment section below the picture I had written one word: *Beautiful.* I had never seen this gorgeous woman look so beautiful. Later, my friend sent me a personal message, which she has given me permission to share:

> Yesterday on Facebook you made a comment I would have never made about myself. In fact, it took me by surprise. You typed "Beautiful" about the picture of me laughing. I almost replied, "I don't think so. I hate the way my nose crinkles up and how my chin looks in this picture." But then I realized your comment is your perception of the picture, not mine. I thought maybe I should consider looking at the photo again. Then I smiled and said a peaceful and sincere "thank-you" to you in my head.

My friend went on to describe her personal battle (and recent small successes) against her cruel inner voice and poor self-image issues. Using her courage as inspiration, I tilted the rearview mirror down one more time. I thought maybe I should reconsider *beautiful* too.

I liked how my cheeks were flushed a peachy rose color from the intensity of my just-completed three-mile run. And how my hair curled into soft waves from the sweltering heat and humidity. I even saw the faintest sparkle in my eyes from the exercise endorphins still radiating through my body.

Beautiful?

That certainly wasn't a word I used to describe myself every day. In fact, I couldn't remember the last time I called myself beautiful.

Maybe never.

It was then that I saw the reflection of two hopeful blue eyes staring back at me. I thought, "Isn't thirty-nine years long enough?"

Isn't thirty-nine years of harsh criticism long enough?

Isn't it time you start seeing beauty in yourself?

And with that, I said a prayer.

At the time, it was for me, but now I believe it is also for you. These healing words are for everyone who yearns to break free from the internal distractions (feelings of shame, guilt, ridicule, insecurity, failure, doubt, and regret) that prevent them from grasping what really matters and truly living.

I wish . . .

I wish you victory against the cruel inner voice,
To see self-acceptance truly is a choice.

I wish you victory against the worries that fill your mind,
To seek contentment that you shall surely find.

I wish you victory against a tunnel vision that blinds your view,
From the exquisite beauty that radiates from you.

I wish you victory against dark thoughts that invade your sleep,
To instead be filled with peace that you shall forever keep.

And through each victory that comes with each passing day,
A melody to fill your heart, for you my friend, I pray.

Loving messages becoming more and more clear,
Drowning out the haunting voice of inner doubt and fear.

And finally you will hear it, and life will truly begin,
The victory song of self-acceptance that only comes from within.

I am not exactly sure what my victory song of self-acceptance will sound like, but I believe it will contain words like *capable*, *brave*, and *strong*. And it will have phrases like "you are enough" and "you are worthy."

I'm quite hopeful I will be hearing a lot of one particular phrase . . .

You are beautiful.

But this time it won't come from a young man in the sunscreen aisle at the drugstore.

From now on, those loving words will come from within.

 ## HANDS FREE WEEKLY INTENTION

Find Your Anchor

The paper doll my daughter made and my collection of hats were invaluable in my process of developing a more positive inner dialogue. The power of these simple objects dawned on me when I read an enlightening suggestion from Jessica Muroff, founder of *The Be Present Project*. Jessica's advice applies to both external and internal distractions:

> *It helps to find an anchor. Something that will snap you out of your daily distractions. You may find that you need more than one anchor. My anchor for my cell phone addiction is the cover my daughter made for me. For my recent birthday, my awesome neighbors made me a frame to create a vision board. It is beautiful and I filled it with things to remind me of my commitment to be present each day. Anchors are great for motivation and encouragement. Discover one that works just for you.**

This week, identify an anchor that symbolizes what you consider to be beautiful, desirable, successful, or healthy, and post it in a visible location. Choose an empowering quote, Scripture verse, affirming phrase, or picture to refer to when you start going down a negative or critical path. For example:

- I am more than my dress size or a number on the scale.
- This too shall pass.
- I will choose love, peace, and forgiveness.
- "I can do all things through Christ who strengthens me" (Philippians 4:13, KJ2000).
- "The most beautiful people we have known are those who have known defeat, known suffering, known struggle, known loss, and have found their way out of the depths. These persons have an

---

*Jessica Muroff. "No Phone Zones," *The Be Present Project, bepresentproject.com/ no-phone-zones/* (December 3, 2012).

> appreciation, a sensitivity, and an understanding of life that fills them with compassion, gentleness, and a deep loving concern. Beautiful people do not just happen."—Elisabeth Kübler-Ross*
>
> By using a positive anchor we can center our focus on the person we want to be and the life we want to live rather than on the unrealistic standard portrayed in the media. Isn't it time to stop buying into the illusion of the "perfect mom," "super dad," or "ideal woman"? So say goodbye to the inner critic. Let the victory song of self-acceptance begin to play, and may it become the constant melody of your Hands Free life.
>
> ---
>
> *Elisabeth Kübler-Ross, *Death: The Final Stage of Growth* (New York: Touchstone, 1975), 93.

ARE YOU FOR REAL?

As I drew closer to the front of the carpool line, my worry grew. Standing next to her teacher was my small child with a desperate look on her face. Something was terribly wrong.

Ushering Avery into the car, the cheerful teacher shared what she thought was a funny incident that happened at lunch. Apparently, my reserved daughter had attempted to shoot a basket with her half-finished yogurt container. When the container hit the bottom of the trash can, the yogurt splashed up, and the whole class laughed hysterically. As soon as the teacher shut the car door, my daughter burst into tears.

"What's wrong, honey?" I asked, knowing full well she felt she'd made a terrible mistake. I could tell she thought the children had laughed *at* her, not with her.

My daughter was too upset to answer my question—she could only cry.

First, I tried to convince her that the children thought it was funny, and they were not laughing at her.

"Don't say that, Mom," she said through tears.

Then I tried to assure her that her teacher was not mad, that in fact, her teacher thought it was funny.

"Stop saying that," Avery said, still clearly distraught.

As I was about to try to reassure her again, I stopped. *She's telling you she's sad—it's okay. Let her cry . . . let her feel sad . . . let her be real.* Instead of continuing to convince and console, I was silent and we listened to her favorite music CD. When we arrived home, she got out of the car and whimpered, "I'm still a little sad."

I simply opened my arms. She collapsed into my hug and sobbed.

That night, Avery and I snuggled in her bed after reading her favorite book. Her eyes filled with tears as she remembered the incident at school.

"I'm still a little sad," she informed me.

I felt compelled not to dismiss her sadness. I simply held her tightly and let her know how much I loved her.

The next morning, Avery came running downstairs. With a look of pure delight and amazement, she happily announced, "I'm not sad anymore!"

I could see it on her face. She was at peace.

I knew exactly why.

My child accepted the feelings she was experiencing, but rather than keeping them pent up inside, she let them out. My daughter beautifully illustrated what it means to live in authenticity: to acknowledge unpleasant feelings, like shame and humiliation, and give voice to them. She then asked someone she trusted to sit with her in her sadness—without smoothing over the negative feelings or brushing them away.

What Avery knew at age four took me almost forty years to learn. When I finally did gain this wisdom, there was a significant shift in my Hands Free journey. I vividly remember the event that nudged me from the dark isolation of secrecy into the shining light of authenticity. I had received unexpected news about Natalie's academic progress and felt blindsided by the information. I knew I could not ignore the fears and uncertainties I was experiencing. I knew I must vocalize my feelings by talking to someone.

I phoned a friend I had only known for about a year, but she had older children and had more experience in the parenting department than I did. As I began to tell her what happened, I unexpectedly burst into tears. Then five words came out of my mouth I had never spoken to myself, let alone to someone else. I said, "I feel like a failure."

Once spoken into the air, I could not take them back. But to my surprise, I did not feel embarrassed or ashamed by my admission. Instead, I felt relieved.

Now let me tell you what my friend *did not* say.

She did not say: *Oh, Rachel, that's ridiculous.*

She did not say: *Come on, don't be silly. You are the farthest thing from a failure.*

She did not say: *You'll feel better about it tomorrow. Now let's talk about something else.*

My friend did not do what I had done so many times to my children and to myself when I was trying to uphold a certain image. Instead my friend spoke these healing words with love and compassion: "I'm so sorry, Rachel." My friend offered her presence and allowed me to be real. Then she said something I did not expect. With vulnerability she whispered, "I felt the same way when it happened to me."

I couldn't believe it. This same heartbreaking news had been given to her about her child a few years ago — this incredible mother who seems to balance it all so effortlessly and so perfectly. I never would have thought.

My friend and I talked for an hour about our experiences. It felt empowering to talk through the situation and not to brush away the torment I was feeling. For once, I didn't plaster a smile on my face and say, "I'm fine."

At the end of the conversation, I felt like a weight had been lifted. I still felt anxious and unprepared for what was ahead, but I no longer felt like a failure. I was not alone.

As I look back at the transformations that took place in my

child and in myself simply by speaking our pain, I realize *this* is yet another reflection of what living is all about . . .

Isn't it when we expose our fears and doubts that they stop looking so scary?

Isn't it when we stop portraying a fake image of our self that we make authentic connections?

Isn't it when we open the doors to our messy souls that the joy, laughter, and love can find its way in?

Isn't it when we show each other our scars that we love each other more?

When we stop holding on to our feelings of discontent, we are finally able to grasp what really matters. Therefore, I plan to live out the rest of my life standing in the light of vulnerability and authenticity—and will embrace anyone who courageously meets me there.

 ## HANDS FREE WEEKLY INTENTION

Speak Your Pain

It is difficult, painful even, to discuss the heartbreaks of parenting. We often withhold information because we think people will judge us or that people will think we are bad parents. But by holding back, we are diminishing our chance to connect with someone who might just surprise us by saying, "I am going through this too. Let's help each other."

For far too long, I pushed away my insecurities, doubts, and fears. Tragically, these suppressed feelings festered until something pushed me over the edge and I ended up exploding at the people I loved the most. But life changed for the better when I shared my pain with a trusted friend. After that initial conversation, my friend and I continued on a path of honesty and authenticity with one another. She has become a trusted companion to whom I can reveal my most negative, unpleasant, and insecure thoughts and feelings. In her, I find acceptance, understanding, and support. Exposing my own hurts has allowed my friend to share her troubles openly with me. With every hurt we exchange, hope is found.

This week, choose a trusted friend and take a risk of vulnerability, by sharing more of your heart than you usually do. If you already have such a friend, thank him or her for supporting you and allowing you to be yourself.

Crossing over from the darkness of secrecy into the loving light of authenticity begins with one step: Speak the fears. Speak the insecurities. Speak the failures. Speak the frustrations. Say them out loud to yourself and then to someone you trust. Because when you're hanging on to the façade that everything is fine when it's not, it's impossible to laugh, love, and live Hands Free.

HANDS FREE REFLECTION

Acceptance
You Deserve a Day

You deserve a day to feel beautiful in your own skin,
A day where body parts are neither too fat nor too thin.
You deserve a day to see your valued presence on this earth,
A day where age, weight, and IQ don't determine your worth.
You deserve a day when you can speak your mind with ease,
A day where lifelong dreams are yours to seize.
You deserve a day where your spirit soars like a red balloon,
A day without judgment or guilt to last for many moons.
You deserve a day to feel good in the place you are,
A day to embrace your imperfections and heal hidden scars.

You deserve a day to feel proud of the life you've made,
A day where regrets and past mistakes permanently fade.
You deserve a day to be loved without restraint,
A day free from being judged a sinner or a saint.
You belong in a valley with pink daffodils beneath your feet.
You belong in an orchard with apples tasty and sweet.
You belong on a hammock with a cold drink in hand.
You belong in a field of sunflowers fragrant and grand.
You belong in the sunshine and never in the rain.
You belong in a place of safety far from misery and pain.
You belong on an island with warm breezes in your hair.
You belong in a quiet sanctuary free from worry and care.
You belong in a place of forgiveness and grace.
You belong with rays of hope shining on your face.
You deserve a day, if not one thousand more,
To be celebrated, appreciated, and lovingly adored.

REFLECTION QUESTIONS

How do you measure your self-worth? How might you alter those standards to be less superficial and more focused on what really matters in life?

Is your inner critic more vocal when you are in certain situations or around particular people? What changes might you make to minimize your exposure to those situations or people? How might you dispel those negative thoughts?

Do other people know the real you? Do you attempt to make things in your life seem better than they actually are? What might happen if you were to reveal your true self and your struggles to a trusted friend?

Chapter 9

REVEAL YOUR TRUE SELF

Authenticity

The thing that is really hard, and really amazing, is giving up
on being perfect and beginning the work of becoming yourself.
Anna Quindlen

SILENCING MY INNER CRITIC ignited a positive change inside me that became more and more apparent each day. As I strode to the park wearing a hat and no makeup, as I declined requests to head up events, as my homemade baked goods were replaced with store-bought pastries, there was a noticeable difference in my actions and my appearance. My type-A overachieving tendencies were slowly disappearing. I wanted nothing more than to continue this Hands Free internal transformation, but I knew there was more letting-go to do. If I truly wanted to be real on the inside, it was necessary to be real on the outside.

When I reached this stage of the journey, it became clear I had wasted too much precious time focusing on what other people think. No longer did I want to miss out on opportunities to enjoy life because I thought someone might disapprove. No longer did

I want to shy away from my dreams because I thought I wasn't good enough. No longer did I want to see my children or myself crumble under unattainable standards of perfection. This step was the catalyst for revealing my authentic self. It was time to show the world the real me—imperfections and all.

As you read the stories in this chapter, I hope you will be inspired to send perfection packing. Through the narratives and weekly intentions, I encourage you to begin developing practices to help you embrace your flaws as well as your children's and to live more authentically and joyfully. I hope you will discover that regardless of the standards you once set for yourself, regardless of what people have come to expect of you, and regardless of how you think you're *supposed* to live, it is not too late to live as the real you.

COME AS YOU ARE

The day had gotten away from me. It was a Hands Free Saturday, which meant having fun took priority over showering and doing my hair. But now it was almost four o'clock, and I was still wearing the same clothes I'd worn in my early morning workout.

I glanced at my unsightly appearance, thinking I should probably change before taking my kids to a neighborhood birthday party. But then I remembered the party was a drop-off party, meaning parents weren't required to stay. While my daughters enjoyed the party, I would have time to run home, grab a shower, and come back looking presentable.

You can only imagine how surprised I was when I pulled up and saw what resembled a small block party in front of the designated house. Because we had just experienced a pleasant cold snap in the South, all the adults had donned their ultra-stylish fall apparel.

As I sunk lower and lower behind the steering wheel, Avery was in the backseat celebrating. "Look! The party is not just for kids! It's for moms and dads too!"

As excitedly as one would announce me as the winner of a million-dollar lottery, Natalie declared, "You can stay, Mama! You can stay!"

My first thought was that I'd rather clean a ten-gallon fish tank with a Barbie toothbrush. I looked down at my attire hoping it wasn't as bad as I thought. The prehistoric workout shorts from the days when step aerobics were popular were still there. The permanent stain on the front of my T-shirt from an exploding pot of spaghetti sauce was still there too. On second glance, my appearance was worse than I had originally thought.

"I thought this was a drop-off party," I mumbled to myself through gritted teeth, unable to open the door and face the ever-growing crowd that appeared to be auditioning for a trendy Gap photo shoot.

Two little faces popped up. "You look fine, Mama," they lovingly said in unison.

I knew my shallow and insecure reaction was not the message I wanted to give my impressionable daughters. I desperately wanted to say, "You're so right! Who cares? So what if I'm little underdressed! I'm going to accompany you to the party and have a great time!"

But I couldn't say those things. I just couldn't. The recent progress I had made to be inwardly loving and accepting toward myself suddenly disappeared when I had to go public with my imperfect outer self.

I pulled down my sweat-stained ball cap as far as it would go and refused to make eye contact with anyone. I made a beeline straight to the hostess and embarrassingly whispered my predicament. After apologizing for not understanding the circumstances of the party, I was assured that it was perfectly fine to leave the children and come back in two hours.

So that was that. I ran back to my car, relieved to simply forget about that small matter and move on. But there was someone who didn't brush it under the rug as I conveniently did. Avery brought up my hasty retreat four days later.

"Melissa's mom had on exercise clothes at the birthday party, Mama. She stayed the whole entire time, and she had fun," my observant child reported as she put her shoes on for school.

I wanted to crawl under the table.

I had totally missed what really mattered that day, and I needed to tell her so.

I bent down and put my hands on her sturdy little shoulders, "Thank you for telling me that. You know what? Melissa's mom was right. It doesn't matter what you have on. You should just *come as you are* and enjoy the experience." Then I hugged her tightly to my chest and added, "I wish I would have stayed. Next time it happens, I will remember 'come as you are' because that is what's important."

"Pinkie promise?" said my freckle-faced girl.

I detected a small quiver in my hand as I held out my pinkie. If such a situation happened to occur again, would I really throw up my hands and say, "Who cares what I look like? I don't want to miss this opportunity!"?

But before such a chance arose, I was presented with undeniable evidence that the "come as you are" approach to life was exactly how I wanted to live.

I was asked to speak about my Hands Free journey at a neighborhood Bible study that country singer Sara Evans regularly attended in the home of one of her friends. In the days leading up to the speaking engagement, my ukulele-playing daughter and I listened to Sara's songs and watched her music videos. Naturally, we wanted to find out all there was to know about this amazingly talented country-music artist. My child and I were captivated by her enormous voice and classic beauty that radiated through an electronic screen.

But I must tell you, Sara Evans is even more beautiful in person.

She exudes kindness, strength, wisdom, faith, and absolute loveliness. She has the kind of soul-deep beauty that immediately draws you into her heart, just like the soothing tone of her singing voice.

But I must tell you why I offered up a silent prayer of gratitude when I first saw Sara. I was expecting her to look like she did in her videos—perfectly polished with every hair in place. But instead, the real Sara showed up. She had on workout clothes, her hair was in a ponytail, and her face was makeup free. I saw her imperfections as clear as day, but they were not unbecoming; they were beautiful. She *was* beautiful.

That's when I finally got the message.

I finally got it loud and clear.

And it sounded like this:

Come as you are.

Come with your hair uncombed.

Come with your misshapen body.

Come with your flat feet and the blemish on your nose.

Come with your wrinkled skin and deep laugh lines.

Come with your inexperience, uncertainty, and inner doubt.

Come with your scars.

Come with your brokenness.

Come with your fears.

Come as you are.

Just come as you are.

And by choosing to come, instead of retreat, you will give yourself a chance to connect, a chance to heal, and a chance to LIVE.

Come as you are and live.

 ## HANDS FREE WEEKLY INTENTION

Come As You Are!

A breakthrough in my journey occurred when my "private self" (the place where my imperfections, insecurities, and fears were openly shared) merged with my "public self" (the persona I presented to the world). It occurred to me that the people I most enjoyed being around and most wanted to emulate were those who openly shared their flaws and shortcomings. They were people who were honest about how difficult life, marriage, and parenthood can be. Not only did I yearn to be surrounded by this Come As You Are genuineness, but I wanted to display this authenticity myself.

On her blog, Brené Brown, author of *The Gifts of Imperfection*, comments on the powerful impact of openly sharing our flawed lives and flawed selves: "Imperfection is not inadequacy—it's what connects us to each other and to our humanity. Vulnerability is not weakness—it's the birthplace of love, creativity, innovation, authenticity and joy."*

Such authenticity is exactly what I want my life and my daughters' lives to look like. I long to surround myself with Come As You Are genuineness for the rest of my life.

Choose one day this week to Come As You Are. This might mean different things to different people, but my suggestion is that you focus solely on enjoying the experience, rather than focusing on your appearance, your qualifications, or whether or not you think you fit in. Being able to "come as you are" means living freely and joyfully, without the damaging constraints of perfectionism. Wouldn't the world be a more loving and accepting place if we could all just Come As We Are? Let this revolutionary approach to life begin with you.

---

*Brené Brown, "Contributions, Criticism and Courage," *Brenebrown.com*, brenebrown.com/2011/1/20/2011120/contributions-criticisms-and-courage.html (January 21, 2011).

THE TICKET IN MY POCKET

I never thought I'd be able to let things happen without a ten-step plan. I never thought I would be able to say my name and the word "spontaneous" in the same sentence. I never thought I'd suggest a bike ride shortly before dinner guests were due to visit our home. But I did.

On Super Bowl Sunday, thirty minutes before friends were scheduled to arrive, I could no longer deny that it was one of those superior weather days—a sunny, perfect-temperature kind of day that rarely happens in February. I thought if I didn't get outside and enjoy at least some part of it that I would feel like I had come home from the county fair with a ticket in my pocket ... like I'd wasted something of value ... like I'd missed my chance for the big prize.

I took a moment to assess the situation.

The children were quietly playing. The area where the party food would be served was minimally prepared. Before I became Hands Free, those two variables would have squelched any chance of a bike ride. Those two variables would have meant putting the final touches on the food, lighting scented candles around the house, and maybe even digging out the fun party napkins and arranging them in an artistic way.

But things are different now, and there was a golden ticket burning a hole in my pocket.

In what felt like an out-of-body experience, I announced to the kids that we were going on a bike ride. The girls immediately ran downstairs. By the looks on their faces, they were concerned about my well-being. Since when did a ponytail and workout pants become Mom's party attire?

But they didn't question it. In fact, given the way they ran so quickly to the garage, it appeared they thought I might change my mind. They grabbed their shoes and helmets and were ready to peddle as fast as their legs could go.

We went to our favorite nearby cul-de-sac where the circular drive created a perfect kid-size cycling track. For fifteen glorious minutes, I cruised alongside Avery while Natalie did loops around us. As if the sunshine radiating on their joyful faces was not enough to confirm my decision to take a bike ride right before the party, what happened next sealed it.

From out of nowhere a dog came bounding into the grassy area where we now were taking a short rest. I hopped to my feet as quickly as a ninja and assumed a defensive mode directly in front of Natalie. I was fully prepared to have my terrified child's arms and legs wrapped around my head and neck. It didn't matter what size or how cute the animal is, *fearful* does not fully describe my child's terror of dogs.

But not today.

Today was different ... in so many ways.

I heard a catch in her breath that unexpectedly expelled with a smile. My daughter watched for a moment as the fat, furry, and extremely happy little dog waved his overgrown and out-of-control hairy tail at her. Then she did something that I thought I would never see. She leaned over and smoothed his hair gently yet confidently.

I leaned in, and in a sugary sweet voice reserved for babies and smiling dogs I posed the question we all were wondering, "Are you having a bad hair day, Little Fur Ball?"

The girls exploded with laughter.

After being happily petted for a few more minutes, this gregarious mound of hair with four tiny legs was summoned back home with dog treats from his owner. Without missing a beat, Little Sister (who often points out that she is *not* afraid of dogs) turned to Big Sister and excitedly exclaimed, "You aren't scared anymore!"

The look on Natalie's face indicated that she suddenly realized just how momentous this occasion truly was. For the first time in her life, a dog charged out unexpectedly and she remained calm and unafraid. I actually saw her stand a little taller as she thought back through what had just happened.

We hopped back on our bikes and headed for home. As the children glanced up from their handlebars and looked at me with loving affection, I shuddered to think about what I could have missed.

If I had spend the last thirty-minute period locating the ideal chip bowl, trying on clothes until I found the perfect outfit, arranging fresh hand towels in the bathroom, preparing one more appetizer, sweeping every last crumb from the floor, the results of those actions would have been tragic.

I would have missed a glorious Sunset Moment.

I would have wasted the chance to make a memory.

I would have gone through this glorious God-given day forfeiting one of the best tickets my pocket has ever held.

If I had chosen perfection over going Hands Free, I would have missed a momentous turning point in my daughter's life.

But thank goodness I didn't.

On this day I let things be just as they were—not fancy, not perfect, just good enough for friends who love me no matter what my hair looks like and no matter if my salsa is homemade or store-bought.

And the result was a Super Bowl Sunday that will go down in the history books for a gal who used every ticket in her pocket and went home with an unforgettable prize.

HANDS FREE WEEKLY INTENTION

Use the Ticket in Your Pocket

Getting distracted from what truly matters in life is an easy thing to do in this high-resolution, high-standard, high-pressured, picture-perfect world we live in. With each new season, we are bombarded with a new slew of gorgeous images of what our home, our children, and our waistline could look like if we do a few "easy" steps. I fell into that trap too many times, and as a result I missed many opportunities to embrace life, have fun, and simply enjoy other people's company.

As I celebrate an authentic life, which includes a messy house, a real body, and realistic standards, I see the life I want to live, not the one society airbrushes for me. I can't help but think this Hands Free approach will be reflected in my daughters' future lives—in the way they connect, love, and build their own memories and traditions.

This week, use the Ticket in Your Pocket by letting go of perfection.

Do you find yourself obsessing over doing things perfectly? Do you feel guilty if you forget something, even though you know it's trivial? Do you find that striving for the illusion that everything is going perfectly leaves you feeling empty and overwhelmed? When people ask you how you manage it all, do you feel like a fraud? If so, I encourage you to surrender the illusion of perfection. Start by letting go of one thing you were going to do today that in the grand scheme of life doesn't really matter. Replace it with an activity that you love to do but never feel like you have the time or energy to do. There's a Ticket in Your Pocket and someone waiting to use it with you. Don't waste it.

Whenever pressure for perfection creeps in, I read these poignant words from Dr. Laura Markham:

> *What if you decided to stop measuring yourself? What if you just accepted yourself in all your imperfect glory, knowing that you'll keep growing, but you'll also wake up irritable some mornings, and forget something important at least once a week, and say exactly the wrong thing on a fairly regular basis?*
>
> *What if you decided that your kids are okay precisely as they are, without you needing to perfect their table manners, make sure their clothes match, or insist they clean their rooms? What if you allowed yourself to just love your kids, your life, and yourself completely—messy imperfection and all?**

*Laura Markham, "Is Your Child Coming Up Short?" *Aha!Parenting.com.* www.ahaparenting.com/_blog/Parenting_Blog/post/No_More_Tiny_Tailors/ (February 12, 2013).

THE RADIANT LIGHT OF AN IMPERFECT CHILD

It was this particular line—where Alexis Stewart describes her life as Martha Stewart's daughter—that struck a chord with me: "Martha does everything better! You can't win. If I didn't do something perfectly, I had to do it again. I grew up with a glue gun pointed at my head."*

*Alexis Stewart and Jennifer Koppelman Hutt, *Whateverland: Learning to Live Here* (New York: Wiley, 2011), n.p.

I remember trying to laugh and say, "How outlandish." But I couldn't.

I remember trying to breathe a sigh of relief and say, "I would never parent my child like that." But I couldn't say that either.

Because grasping what matters is not always easy.

Grasping what matters means looking deep inside the soul and admitting hard truths.

And in this case, grasping what matters meant considering whether or not I created a dark shadow of parenting perfectionism upon my children from time to time.

Because let's face it, one would have to live on an isolated island to escape the pressure of having a child who excels at something. Parents are constantly bombarded with opportunities to make their kids smarter, faster, prettier, fitter, and stronger—not to mention more creative, more musical, more artistic, more sociable, and more successful.

We certainly don't want our child to be left behind.

We don't want our child to be chosen last.

We want our child to be "good" at something.

So we push.

We criticize.

We control.

And we demand things of our children that were never demanded of us when we were young.

While many extracurricular activities are healthy and promote positive life-long habits, there is something unhealthy about a screaming parent who is upset because his or her child missed the fly ball, came in third instead of first, or received 90 percent instead of 100 percent on the spelling test.

You see, sometimes kids make mistakes. Sometimes kids get distracted. Sometimes kids just want to play and have fun. Sometimes kids just want to be kids.

Sometimes kids just want to be loved "as is."

How do I know?

I was given this message from a highly reliable source. It didn't come from a well-meaning friend, experienced pediatrician, or renowned child psychology expert. No, this critical message came straight from my child's mouth. As much as it pains me to put this on record, I share it in an effort to spare a child from living one more day under the unachievable standard of perfection.

This is my story ...

Avery was diligently practicing her ukulele for her upcoming music recital. The concert was a few days away. As she practiced, the chords were off-key. Her fingers clumsily searched for proper placement and often neglected to find their home. Her guitar pick was making an excruciating clicking sound. She strummed as though she had never played a note in her life. The only thing I could think about was how disappointing it would be to have her perform so poorly at the concert. So I made her play the recital piece over and over, saying she could do better each time.

After several renditions and little improvement, my child simply laid down her instrument as if surrendering to an unwinnable battle. I watched as tears began to collect on the rims of her eyes before their heaviness caused them to spill in prominent streaks along her cheeks.

Avery's face held the look of defeat. She knew she had not pleased me — and perhaps never could. In a pleading tone of desperation, she spoke seven words I will never forget. "Mama, I just want to be good."

And then once more in case I missed it the first time, "I just want to be good."

My baby, who was trying the best she could to play a complicated instrument, thought she was no good. The act of playing the ukulele, something that had initially brought her so much joy, was now a source of frustration and failure. What she once called her God-given gift was now something she felt she did poorly.

Now where could she have gotten that idea?

Could it have been from all the disapproving looks and constant corrections?

Could it have been from the exasperated breathing coming from the unsmiling lady standing over her?

I felt so ashamed—like a bully who had targeted the same child in the school cafeteria until the child fell to his knees and surrendered every penny in his pocket.

By now, we were both crying.

I never wanted my child to think she was only as good as her accomplishments. I wanted her self-worth to come from who she is, not what she does. Yet that was not the message I had been conveying over the course of our daily practice sessions.

I cradled my daughter in my arms and told her how sorry I was. While I rocked her back and forth, the words of my sensible, laid-back husband came to me in full force. Every time I had vocalized my worry about my child's musical performance in the past, he repeated the same wise words: "She's just a little kid. She loves music and loves playing the ukulele. Just let her have fun. Let her strum and sing her heart out. Who cares what it sounds like?"

Who cares?

That would be me. It was me who cared how she sounded—but I cared too much and for all the wrong reasons. I cared about how it would "look." I cared for my own selfish affirmations. And in the process, I managed to snuff out that beautiful light inside my child that shines when she is doing something she loves because it makes her happy, not because she wants to impress anyone.

By the grace of God, things changed after that pivotal moment. The Mistake Monitor was fired for ukulele practice and The Loving Encourager was hired. Now my daughter and I sit on the front porch for practice time. She plays to the birds, the clouds, and to the evening sun when it kindly graces us with its presence. The birds don't seem to mind the off-key notes and neither do I. Because there's something quite beautiful about a song in its natural, imperfect form. Kind of like the light of joy that radiates on a child's face when she's loved "as is."

When you're tuned in to what really matters, the sound of happiness triumphs over perfect chords. Let joyful imperfection be the chorus of our lives.

HANDS FREE WEEKLY INTENTION

Use "I Love to Watch You _____."

The feedback I gave my child at the conclusion of her performances changed after reading an article by sportswriter Steve Henson. The article, which described powerful insights gathered over three decades by Bruce E. Brown and Rob Miller of Proactive Coaching LLC, contained this unforgettable line: "When hundreds of college and professional athletes were asked what their parents said that made them feel great, that amplified their joy during and after a ball game, their overwhelming response: 'I love to watch you play.'"*

As I adopted the practice of keeping verbiage to a minimum, the reaction on my child's face confirmed my new approach. The joy I saw on her face inspired me to reevaluate the standards I had previously set for my family. Meaningful connection with the people who matter surpassed my need for approval from those who didn't matter.

This week, when providing feedback about your child's performance, use only these six words: "I love to watch you _____."

The next time you feel the need to guide, instruct, or criticize after a ball game, performance, or extracurricular activity, keep it simple instead. Allow your child's coaches and teachers to give needed instruction. And should you become emotional simply by watching someone you love in action, tell him or her. But remember, less is more. Less can be exactly what they need to hear ... no pressure ... just love, pure and simple.

---

*Steve Henson, "What Makes a Nightmare Sports Parent—and What Makes a Great One," *www.thepostgame.com. www.thepostgame.com/blog/more-family-fun/201202/what-makes-nightmare-sports-parent* (February 15, 2012).

 ## HANDS FREE REFLECTION

Authenticity
Waiting for Perfect

After finding a simple bread recipe in her kids' cookbook, my daughter asked with eager eyes if she could make mini loaves for her teacher.

"Right now?" I asked with trepidation. For various shallow and meaningless reasons, "now" was not the ideal time for the kitchen to become an experimental baking lab with dirty bowls, licked spoons, and empty containers.

But there she stood, with the recipe book open as wide as her smile. *If not now, when?* I asked myself. *I mean, come on. Will there ever be a perfect time?*

"Okay, you can try the recipe," I said, smiling at my unconventional-looking baker with mismatched socks and disheveled hair.

And although my independent child was highly capable of making the bread by herself, I asked if I could help. I even rolled up my sleeves and pressed my hands inside the bowl next to hers to help knead the gooey substance.

The counter became coated with flour. A bounty of ingredients lined our work area like a row of disorderly soldiers. The kitchen was a mess. We were a mess! But we laughed. Oh, how my daughter and I laughed as we kneaded that dough!

Eventually, the loaves came out of the oven. They were not pretty; they were misshapen and heavy as bricks. But to my surprise, they tasted heavenly.

And when I saw the way my daughter looked admiringly at the fruits of her labor, I had to fight back the tears.

Not long ago, my need to maintain a picture-perfect image would have prevented this baking session from ever happening—and if somehow it *did* manage to happen, the loaves would have been too unsightly to give as gifts. I would have had to replace them with perfectly plump loaves of bakery bread.

And in the process, I would have missed it all—my child's flour-dusted nose, the tune she hummed while she worked, and the hug in the light of the afternoon sun as it shone through the kitchen window.

Waiting for the perfect time and perfect conditions means waiting to live.

If not now, when?

A beautifully flawed and gratitude-filled life is at our fingertips. But we must roll up our sleeves and dig in—dig into the gooey, heavenly mess that is life.

And when we make the choice to let go of distraction, perfection, and societal pressure to grasp what really matters, that's when our life—although a bit unbalanced and imperfect—tastes sweeter than we could ever imagine.

REFLECTION QUESTIONS

How could you adopt a more Come As You Are approach to life? How might this be beneficial to your children, your spouse, and your friends?

Do you pressure your children to look or perform a certain way? What might happen if you adopt the role of Loving Encourager and accept them "as is"? Would you be willing to try it for a month and see what happens?

Chapter 10

LET GO

Forgiveness

The beauty of life is, while we cannot undo what is done, we can see it, understand it, learn from it and change. So that every new moment is spent not in regret, guilt, fear or anger, but in wisdom, understanding and love.

Jennifer Edwards

TRUTH BE TOLD, I harbored a great deal of guilt for the missed opportunities that occurred during the two years of my highly distracted life. It wasn't until I began living more authentically and silenced my inner critic that I realized the damaging effects of harboring these feelings of regret. By refusing to forgive myself for missing many precious moments in the past, I was sabotaging my chances of grasping the precious moments *today*. Each time I went to that debilitating place of remorse, I was unable to grasp the gifts standing right in front of me. What a foolish waste of time! Plus, I realized that the daily guilt I felt whenever I momentarily slipped back into former bad habits also prevented me from living a present and joy-filled life.

This realization occurred to me one particularly challenging afternoon as the children's bickering and the pressures of everyday life seemed to mount with each passing minute. Through clenched teeth I told my children I needed a moment to myself. Even before I reached my bedroom I knew where my mind would go. Every time I felt like I was failing miserably in the parenting department, I would return to the past—drudging up one bad choice after another until I blamed myself for everything going wrong in that particular moment.

But that day I did something different. I turned to God and thanked him for his graces with me. I thanked him for allowing me to see the error of my distracted ways and begin new practices with my life. Finally, and perhaps most importantly, I asked for the wisdom and strength to let go of those past mistakes and live only in today.

With a newfound sense of hope, I was able to take the next step in my Hands Free journey. I began shifting my focus from negative past and current behaviors to *positive* ones. I told myself, "Yes, I made a mistake, but I choose to focus on what I'm doing right." Rather than paralyzing myself in a state of shame and anguish, this new positive mind-set helped me get back on track after small missteps in my journey.

It soon became apparent that by extending grace to myself, I was able to offer it more readily to my children and spouse. I found myself apologizing more often and was able to openly admit sorrow for past wrongdoings. Not only was this a healing practice for myself, but it also provided a healthy and loving model for my children to use as they made their own mistakes.

The stories in this chapter explore the liberating truth that living Hands Free is not about what happened yesterday; it is about today. Letting go of past mistakes is an integral part of the Hands Free journey because it allows the gifts of the present day to become more apparent. By sharing my own struggles to accept grace, I hope you will be empowered to let go of past mistakes and long-standing regrets—and that you will learn to focus on what you *can* control: your actions and choices in the present day.

MOMENT OF IMPACT

It's funny the things kids remember.

This thought dawned on me as I put conditioner on Avery's freshly shampooed hair. She reminded me to leave the conditioner on for five minutes so her hair would be extra curly. I shook my head in amazement knowing this tidbit was something her aunt had told her almost a year earlier.

I set the timer on my watch and placed my hand under my chin as my daughter continued to play in the tub. While thick droplets of conditioner made ripples in the bathwater, she began to talk. What spilled out was a memory from the height of my distracted life that had been waiting to surface. Nothing could have prepared me for her painful recollection.

Avery, who was three years old at the time, remembered arriving at a holiday event in our community only to be forced to leave immediately. She remembered I was angry, that I started crying, and that my friend walked outside the building to comfort me. She remembered my friend saying, "Mommies sometimes need a little time to be alone and take a deep breath."

What my daughter *did not* remember was that her father had been traveling for work several weeks in a row, that I had just discovered her sister's third case of head lice in a two-month time period, and that the new shoes she and her sister were wearing were producing blisters—and they were whining.

My daughter did not remember those things. Her only recollection was that I was yelling, crying, and we could not stay at the fun party because I was falling apart. She remembered that I could not save myself from this troubled state—that another adult had to rescue me.

As my child recounted this devastating memory in minute detail, my mouth hung open in disbelief. The only reason I did not start to cry was because I was so awestruck by her remarkable recall.

All this turmoil had been tucked away since she was three years old.

Of course, I knew exactly what night she was talking about. I remember hating the woman I was at that moment—the woman who was allowing lice and blisters to steal her joy. I was the woman who couldn't quite get ahold of herself and acknowledge these were not true "problems"—that things could be much, much worse.

But that is precisely what distraction overload will do. It robs you of your sensibility ... distorts what is truly important ... causes you to focus on details that won't matter in one year or even tomorrow. Distraction overload slowly begins to unravel the fabric of your well-being until one day you come completely undone.

And you can only stand there watching it happen. Because you can't save yourself.

That night, I was dying. I was buried beneath the chaos of my life, which I had created by being overly tied to my phone, computer, and bulging daily planner—by saying yes to too many meaningless commitments and not enough yeses to what really mattered.

My dear friend helped me gather myself so we could go back to the party and attempt to grasp a small shred of joy in a shattered evening. I remember walking behind my loving friend, watching her hold Avery's hand, even managing to get her to smile. I was thinking to myself, "I am glad that's over. No damage done."

Who was I kidding?

I left an imprint that night, a tender red mark on my child's impressionable soul—a mark I would not see until a summer evening several years later when the smell of hair conditioner triggered an agonizing moment in her young life.

As my child reflected back on that night, vivid details spilled from her lips as if the incident happened yesterday. She was clearly surprised by her own emotional reaction, blinking back the tears and saying with embarrassment, "I can't believe this is making me cry."

I painfully watched her struggle to maintain her composure, and all I could think was this:

Never again will I wonder if the harsh tone of my voice is absorbed into small ears and tender spirits ...

Never again will I wonder if my angry words are retained in young souls ...

Never again will I wonder if the bad memories are cataloged right along with the good in her memory bank ...

Because now I know.

But this story is not over. This story is not about guilt, shame, or regret over things a person cannot change.

This story is about hope.

Because what happened next is pivotal.

I looked into my child's face and said the *only* words that could be said to a child who remembered the harsh words and actions of an overwhelmed mother three years before.

"I am sorry. I am so very sorry. Will you forgive me?"

And then right before my very eyes, I saw a transformation take place in my child—from a wounded soul to a hopeful survivor with a chance at a beautiful future. My child threw her whole body into her act of forgiveness by wrapping her arms tightly around my neck and whispering, "Oh yes, Mama. I forgive you."

Like there was never any doubt.

But there was more. I needed her to know I was handling stress and frustration differently now. Because the truth is this: even though I am no longer living a highly distracted life, parenting is hard—sometimes downright impossible. And I can sense when a collision is coming—when sibling bickering, messy bedroom floors, and bad attitudes are about to collide with my foul mood, my sleep-deprived state of mind, or my threadbare patience. And when those factors intersect, that moment of impact cannot be undone.

So just like a driver who is anticipating a damaging collision with another vehicle, I let off the gas … I pull back … I pause to avoid permanent damage.

In those moments when I am about to yell or explode, I remain silent just long enough for the angry words to dissipate. I hold the words under my tongue for just a few moments until the moment has passed. I have discovered that even a few seconds of pause can prevent tragic results.

The moment of impact …

Is there anything we wouldn't do to prevent hurtful words spilling from our lips—leaving tender marks on those we love the most?

The moment of impact …

175

Is there anything we wouldn't do to save ourselves from years of painful regret, remorse, and shame?

The moment of impact . . .

Sometimes it just takes a pause to avoid a collision.

My daughter and I concluded our discussion, and I gently tucked her into bed. As I was about to close her bedroom door, she called out the same question she has asked every night since she could talk: "Where will you be, Mama?"

Normally I tell her what part of the house I will be in, but that night I added one more detail of assurance.

"I will be here for you, sweet girl."

I will be here.

I can't go back and change the past, but I can do something about now—now when my children are depending on me to be here for them when they need a safe, consistent environment and a loving support system.

By the grace of God, I am trying to do things differently now.

When the collisions of life are upon me, I look at my children's faces and remember that what I say and do in that moment might very well be with them forever.

And in that brief moment of pause—just before the moment of impact—my precious children have the power to save me from myself.

 ## HANDS FREE WEEKLY INTENTION

Offer Yourself Grace

Assessing the cost of my distracted ways was critical to changing my behavior, but living in regret over missed opportunities was not. I finally came to a point when I realized that continually berating myself over lost moments was a waste of precious time and energy. Self-forgiveness became just as important to my Hands Free life transformation as recognizing the cost of my distraction was at the beginning of the journey.

I realized that the moments I raised my voice at my children had little to do with them and a lot to do with me. I was more likely to become angry in moments when I felt like I was failing as a parent, either for a mistake I made on that particular day or had made in the past. When I began to pause and hold those angry words under my tongue for a moment, I was reminded of the power of grace. The One who loves me even when I fail miserably reminded me that even the best parents have their moments of self-doubt and frustration. In those moments of pause, I felt God's loving presence assuring me that he loves me unconditionally. By accepting God's grace, I was able to offer myself grace in times of anger and shame—and it trickled down to my children and impacted their lives in countless ways.

This week, avoid causing damaging moments of impact with the people you love by pausing for a few moments and offering yourself grace. When dinner burns . . . when the jeans won't quite button . . . when you forget something important and feel like you've let others down, give yourself a moment. Remind yourself you are human and doing the best you can.

By taking a moment when the collusions of life are upon you, you and your loved ones can reap the benefits of a mindful pause:

- It can prevent you from saying hurtful words.
- It can keep you from leaving marks on the tender souls of those you love.
- It can spare you from years of painful regret and shame.

When a moment of impact is looming, pause, offer yourself grace, and provide a calm and reasoned response.

THE HERO INSIDE YOU

Throughout the day, local newscasters advised my entire viewing area to prepare for life-threatening weather. Forecasters pronounced the word *tornado* as if it were vile profanity. After all, the wounds were still fresh from the devastation caused by a mile-wide tornado that claimed the lives of 316 people in my state just ten months before.

Children were released early from school and many businesses closed. Grocery stores were packed with people buying nonperishable food, bottled water, and batteries. But by seven o'clock that evening, it appeared we would be spared as the severe weather headed north of us.

After consulting multiple weather reports, my husband and I decided that it was safe for our daughters to sleep in their upstairs bedrooms as usual. As we tucked them into bed, fear covered their faces like the blue tarps that still remained on some of the damaged houses in our community. My children had done their part to help those who had lost family members and homes in our state's deadly storm. But as a result, they knew all too well the merciless wrath of a tornado.

Natalie was especially anxious and asked me to stay with her. After two hours of watching her eyes pop open at the slightest hint of wind or rain, she finally succumbed to sleep. I carefully crept out of her room, checked the radar, and began my decent downstairs to my bedroom.

But I only made it down two steps when I was frozen in my tracks. As if stuck in hardened cement, my feet refused to move. My eyes darted to the window nearby. I watched as trees violently swayed and sheets of rain ricocheted off our neighbor's roof.

"I can't go downstairs," I whispered to the dark shadows.

I took a deep breath to calm myself. The rational part of me knew I had just checked the radar and the weather radio was turned on. Yet all I could think about was how quickly and unexpectedly an F2 tornado had come upon us less than a year before. I knew with certainty that if I went downstairs and suddenly needed to protect my children, I would not make it in time.

With that sobering thought, I turned around and went back to Natalie's room. I gently laid myself down in the indented spot in the bed next to my sleeping child. It was still warm from where my body had rested just minutes before.

Perhaps you are familiar with the tendency of one's mind to go to the darkest, strangest, most irrational places in the wee hours of the night. If you are, then you can imagine the bleak road on which my mind then traveled.

I began playing out all the possible life-saving scenarios in the event that I heard the unmistakable sound of a tornado. In all the scenarios, I never once let go of my children—even if it meant being blown upward into the deadly vortex. I was resigned to the fact that if they were going to die, I was going to die with them. Actually, there was nowhere else I would rather be in their final hours.

Suddenly, the magnitude of this sacrificial thought hit me. A divine whisper of affirmation instantly popped into my head:

You are a good mom.

And then again; this time a little louder.

You are a good mom.

Silent, warm tears slid from the corners of my eyes onto my child's yellow pillowcase. I knew exactly why those words touched me so deeply. Because I don't say them often enough. In fact, I couldn't remember the last time I said them to myself. Truth be told, I often find myself saying the complete opposite.

The gentle voice inside me that said, *"You are a good mom,"* had more healing words to offer ...

So you aren't perfect. You make mistakes and even some poor choices. Some days your patience is too thin ... some days you allow negative thoughts to silence thoughts of gratitude ... some days you aren't the mom you want to be.

But hear this, and remember it:

When your children need defending, you defend.

When your children need comfort, you comfort.

When your children hurt, you hurt too.

And the reason you lie here wide awake when you could be sleeping soundly in your own bed is because you are willing to die for them.

So stop berating yourself.

Stop questioning yourself.

Stop shaming yourself.

And for God's sake, stop criticizing yourself.

Stop wondering if you are enough.

Because you are.

The fact that you have vowed to take on any monster of nature or human form that threatens your children overshadows the daily mistakes you make as a parent.

It is time to let go of the guilt and live each passing day knowing the love you have for your children is a life-sustaining positive that surmounts all the other negatives.

And with that, the providential lecture was over.

Although I initially experienced it as a divine reprimand, it also gave me great comfort. In fact, I expelled a long, heavy sigh and was able to close my eyes peacefully in a way I hadn't for quite some time — perhaps since my first child was born almost a decade earlier.

A few hours later, promising rays of sunlight poked through the shutters. Although my heavy eyes longed for more sleep, my spirit felt renewed. Just like the light of a new day, I felt hopeful. I repeated those five beautifully healing words in my head over and over: *You are a good mom.*

Slowly my daughter rolled over, and her sleepy brown eyes registered a look of surprise — surprise that I was still there beside her.

Natalie smiled slowly and quietly whispered words of gratitude, "Thank you for staying with me all night, Mama." And then she looked at me in a way I had never noticed before — the way survivors regard their heroes who risked life and limb to save them.

A new day has begun. Life is too short for guilt and condemnation. I have a life to live and people to love and protect. I am a hero to two little girls ... it's time I start treating myself like one.

 ## HANDS FREE WEEKLY INTENTION

Create (or Maintain) a Distraction-Free Daily Ritual

Natalie first requested Talk Time when she was three years old. From there, it became a sacred, nightly ritual that occurred after a storybook was read. For ten minutes, we cuddled in the dark and no topic of discussion was off limits. This special time has continued without fail ever since, even throughout my highly distracted, overly committed years. There were only a handful of nights that I missed Talk Time, and on those nights, I felt unsettled. I have come to enjoy and rely on Talk Time just as much as my child.

No matter how miserably I have failed in the parenting department on a particular day, Talk Time gives me the chance to offer my loving presence, my undivided attention, and my heartfelt apologies. Meaningful family rituals, like Talk Time, provide a chance to start again.

This week, create (or maintain) one Daily Ritual where time with your loved one is protected from all distraction and interruption. Choose one of the following Daily Rituals to implement (or maintain) in your life, or create your own.

- Morning snuggles
- Nightly tuck-in
- Walking the dog or caring for a pet together
- Prayer time or daily devotional
- After-school snack time

The key is to do it every day so that no matter how chaotic the day is, your child can always count on that one period of meaningful connection.

You will find that establishing a special time of connection with a loved one each day has immeasurable rewards. Not only does this routine activity build a foundation for your current and future relationship, but it also provides a redeeming action that you can focus and rely on when you stumble on your journey. Life is too short for guilt and condemnation; find peace in an everyday family ritual.

A DESCRIPTION FOR HEALING

Perhaps the most promising aspect of living Hands Free is that it is not about what happened yesterday—it is about *today* and the critical choices we make now.

But there are times when I must look back.

Every time I'm invited to speak to a new group about my Hands Free journey, I have to go there—to the past. Sharing my story means drudging up old wounds that are difficult to relive, let alone speak out loud.

There is one particular part of my story that is especially hard to divulge. In fact, I am unable to say these words without my voice catching and a tear sliding down the side of my face:

> Excessive phone use, commitment overload, multiple page to-do lists, and the pursuit of perfection consumed me. And yelling at the people I loved was a direct result of the loss of control I was feeling in my life. Inevitably, I had to fall apart somewhere. So I fell apart behind closed doors in the company of the people who meant the most to me.

I shudder when I reflect on the person my distraction overload caused me to be. Yet I am often reminded that my past, particularly my highly distracted years, made me who I am today. When I occasionally regress to my old ways, that sickening wave of déjà vu causes me to feel grateful for how far I've come.

So when I saw this interesting idea at *www.justbeenough.com*, I was intrigued. If I asked my children to describe me in three words, what would they say? I prayed the words *grumpy, impatient,* or *mean* wouldn't tumble from their lips. I prayed the terms *too busy* or *drill sergeant* wouldn't be perfect descriptors for me. I also hoped neither of my children would timidly say something like, "You use the words 'hurry up' a lot." Because that is how it used to be.

So at the conclusion of our nightly Talk Time one evening, I asked Natalie to write down three words that describe me. As she wrote, I eagerly studied each stroke of her pen as if she were disclosing a homemade remedy for saggy eyelids or the undiscovered recipe for calorie-free chocolate truffles.

This is what she wrote: "Nice ... friendly ... caring." And at the bottom of the list, "Best mom in the world!"

I stared at that piece of paper with a big goofy smile just as I did when I saw my first official teaching license at the ripe old age of twenty-two.

Then I hurried into Avery's room, eager to see if she would have an equally positive list. She didn't understand what the word *describe* meant, so I said, "If someone asked, 'What is your mom like?' what would you say?"

As her eyes rolled upward into thinking position, I stared at her little pink lips anxiously awaiting her response. After all, *she* was the child who bore the brunt of my distracted ways—being impatiently schlepped around and taking second place to incoming emails, text messages, and massive to-do lists while her older sister was in school.

Finally my curly-haired daughter spoke.

"Pretty ... kind ... nice."

Whew. I felt a mixture of relief and redemption at the positive descriptions I'd received from both of my children. But before I could release an entire celebratory breath, I jumped to a new inquiry. The drill sergeant, control freak, type-A part of me that occasionally rears its ugly head was not quite satisfied. That competitive part of me wondered how my children would describe their dad. After all, he is and always has been the epitome of Hands Free—freely letting go of his electronic devices once he walks in the door from work and freely letting go of anger, grudges, and mistakes. My husband certainly never had to have a breakdown-breakthrough moment to get his priorities straight. He is consistently even, laid-back, and calm. How would my children describe *him*?

I went back to Natalie's room and asked her.

She said: "Happy ... adventurous ... nice ... jumpy." She then defined *jumpy* as "likes to get up and do stuff."

Then I went to Avery's room. She too could not be limited to three descriptors for her dad. She said: "Nice ... tickles me ... plays tackle ... really fun."

I must admit, I was jealous. My list was good; actually, it was wonderful. (It sure beats *unhappy*, *grouchy*, and *stressed out*, which is what my list would have been in my Non–Hands Free days.) But I'll be honest, I wanted words like *fun*, *happy*, and *adventurous* on *my* list. So I decided to take a cue from their naturally Hands Free dad and began taking the "letting go" part of the Hands Free equation to its maximum potential. Within a few weeks' time, I had offered these Hands Free efforts:

- I suggested we let the dishes go and run outside in the rain. I didn't touch worms, but I did jump in a mud puddle.
- I initiated a game of front-yard tag after the kids put on their pajamas. I was not fast enough to catch them, but they sure delighted in seeing me try.
- I roller-skated for the first time in ten years and didn't embarrass myself with klutzy moves or dangerous collisions.
- I announced a spontaneous picnic despite the fact that we had no picnic-type foods in the house.
- I tossed the football and played a round of kickball all in one day. No one cared one bit that my aim was atrocious, even Avery, who I accidently hit on the nose with the ball.

I'll admit, I had not participated in some of those activities since I was a child. My overly cautious nature often prevents me from jumping into activities with no hesitation. But being spontaneous and playful created a tangible connection to my children that simply observing them did not. I vowed to continue jumping in with gusto as often as I could.

But I couldn't leave it at that—I just had to know.

Did my heightened level of adventure and spontaneity improve my image? Would I now be among the elite adults who fell into the "fun" category like their father and beloved uncle? That evening, after Avery's two-book ritual and Talk Time, I went for it.

"If someone didn't know me and asked you, 'What is your mom like?' what would you say?"

The first response from my clever child who apparently does not like to play this game twice was, "We already talked about this."

But after sweetly requesting she answer it again, she obliged. I sucked in my breath and mentally willed the word *fun* to pop out of her mouth.

She replied, "Pretty … nice … kind."

Although there was a slight difference in order from the initial list, Avery's description of me hadn't changed one bit. But before I could even be the least bit disappointed, I swear she looked straight into my soul and added something I so desperately needed to hear.

"When I see you, I think of how we read together every night. I think of how you take care of me. I think about how you love me and have always loved me."

I couldn't help it—two fat tears slid down my face, one on each side. This beautiful description of me came from the child who was once ignored by her stretched-too-thin mother. These words came from the child who was once given the worthless leftover scraps of my highly distracted life.

And suddenly I had an epiphany that was long overdue.

Maybe it's time I stop feeling guilty for the moments I missed with my children.

Maybe it's time I stop crying when I think back on those misguided years.

Maybe it's time I acknowledge that I am a good mother, and, despite the fact that for two years I lost my way, I never stopped loving them.

But above all else, there was one profound realization that finally registered in my tormented mind:

Those who I wronged have forgiven me. Maybe it's time I forgive myself.

HANDS FREE WEEKLY INTENTION

Ask for Three Words

When I see tears quietly streaming down the faces of those who listen to my painful journey to grasp what really matters, I find it difficult to speak. I have come to the realization that being a parent is much harder than society allows us to acknowledge. When we strip it down to the raw, tender places in our soul, we find guilt, uncertainty, judgment, and regret. Part of what has helped me in my quest for self-forgiveness is to know that I am not alone. When a reader of my blog shared her powerful story about self-forgiveness, I was greatly comforted. I refer to her story often to remind myself what is truly important:

> *I lived the first few years of my daughter's life distracted and scared. With all of her therapies and uncertainty about her future, I was a mess. I withdrew from friends because it was just too hard to be around other "normal" kids when mine was so far behind. And while I was loving and attentive with my daughter, my fear came out as anger toward my son. I had no patience with him and incredibly high expectations. Looking back, I try to tell myself that we did have good bonding moments during this time because we did; but it is the period of my life that I call "my crazy, angry mommy days." Our house was not a happy place, and mommy wasn't a safe and happy person for my son. I can't explain the guilt I feel when I look back. I regularly ask myself when I am going to let these feelings go, as it was long ago and I am not in that place anymore. But it is so hard to let the guilt go. Your journey has helped my journey more than you can know, as I feel the incredible need to make each moment count and be there for my kids, especially because I don't feel that I could do that during those times. So tonight, I'm going to hold my breath and ask my children the "three words to describe me" question*

when I put them to bed. And, as long as "crazy" isn't a word they use to describe me, I'm going to try to celebrate how far we've come instead of regretting that I ever lost sight of the amazing blessing that both of my children are and how precious this time with them is.

Ask someone you love and trust for three words to describe you. Their words might surprise you. They might also heal you. Perhaps it's time to stop beating yourself up over past mistakes. Perhaps it's time to stop reliving your personal failures thinking others are holding a grudge against you. Perhaps it is just *you.* Perhaps those who love you look at you and see the positively wonderful things that you are. Maybe it's time to look forward and stop looking back.

HANDS FREE REFLECTION

Forgiveness
Free from the Heavy

There are days when we want to beat our head against the wall, when we scream into our pillow and leave tears upon the steering wheel.

There are days when we feel there is no more left to give, when we want to throw in the towel and admit, "I can't do this anymore."

There are days when the words spoken in our head are words we never want another soul to hear.

There are days when we feel like we've made too many mistakes to ever be redeemed.

Those days are not pretty.

But despite the failure, the missteps, the doubt, and inner turmoil we experience, we do something extraordinary.

We show up.

And we keep showing up.

Because we know someone is counting on us.

And when that someone sees us showing up, it means more than we even know.

Then one day, maybe sooner that we think, every sacrifice we ever made and every tear we ever cried will be exchanged for something wondrous.

Maybe it will be a tender word, an apologetic embrace, an expression of joy—whatever it is, we will know because it is the moment we have been waiting for, perhaps praying for.

In that moment we will shine at the one we love and the one we love will shine back at us.

And every past mistake that once weighed heavily on our soul will be overshadowed by the light of a beautiful moment in time.

And at last we will be free from the heavy.

REFLECTION QUESTIONS

Are there certain past mistakes that you continually relive? Is there anything you can do to rectify those mistakes now? If not, what might you say to yourself about the lessons learned from those mistakes as a way of offering yourself grace?

Does your family have a daily ritual in place that brings peace, calm, and connection in the midst of (or at the end of) a challenging day? If not, what daily ritual would you like to establish and how will you implement it?

When you raise your voice at your loved ones, what thoughts go through your head? Is your anger ever misdirected? What might you say to yourself in these moments of stress and frustration to prevent yourself from saying or doing something you might later regret?

Chapter 11

SEIZE THE CALLINGS OF YOUR HEART

Compassion

How do you say "thank you" for sunshine or health . . . for clear days or gentle rains . . . for happiness, joy or love? You say it by sharing what you have. You say it by making the world a better place in which to live.

Thomas D. Willhite

I CAN PINPOINT THE TIMES when I felt most at peace and most grateful for the blessings in my life. It was when I was engaging in small acts of kindness without expecting anything in return. As a child and young adult, I often wrote special poems and notes of appreciation to people I cared about. I loved surprising friends and family with baked goods or a special playlist on a CD. But most of all, I loved saying yes to the urgings of my heart when I saw someone who was hurting. My distracted years pulled me away from this mindful practice of giving, and I lost sight of my true passions. While there were plenty of opportunities to help others, I failed to be selective. Saying yes to every service opportunity that came my way meant saying no to the callings of my heart.

189

And every time I did, I felt unsettled—as if I were missing a key ingredient to a fulfilling life.

Once I had a good handle on both the *external* and *internal* distractions in my life, I knew the next step I needed to take on my journey. From past experience, I knew that performing small acts of kindness from the heart was the essence of grasping what really matters. Once again, I needed to get in touch with my true passions and then act on them. I wanted to make a difference in the world, and I wanted to raise children who wanted to make a difference in the world. Perhaps such a lofty goal sounds grandiose and maybe even impossible, but I found that it was not. Making a difference in the world on the Hands Free journey meant making a difference in one life. One life. That is all.

In this chapter, I share a few of my most impactful gifting experiences that illustrate how individuals and families can let go of daily distraction to touch another person's life. As you reflect on the stories and engage in the weekly intentions, I invite you to enrich your life and your children's lives by acting on the callings of your heart.

THE CLEAN LINES OF A LOVING HEART

On Valentine's Day every year, my family and I covered all the usual people that one would think of as a "valentine," such as teachers, close friends, and family members. But on my first ever Hands Free Valentine's Day, I felt compelled to go beyond our usual circle.

As I considered how to do this, a question came to mind: What is the total opposite of pink and red flowers, colorful heart-shaped boxes, mushy words of love, and hugs and kisses? The answer was *trash*—dirty, smelly, unsightly, unwanted trash.

As unpleasant as it was to think about garbage, I needed to acknowledge the fact that there were some hardworking folks in my life who made it magically disappear. How often had I taken that significant detail for granted?

Even if the temperature outside were cold enough to freeze nose hairs ... even if the diaper-filled canister could be smelled beyond a ten-mile radius ... even if my bulging trash container held rotted pumpkins or prickly Christmas trees, my disgusting rubbish was always taken away.

The demanding physical duties of my trash collectors had crossed my mind a few times in the past. Yet every time I thought about doing something nice for them, I'd get sidetracked. My good intentions had a way of vanishing, just like the waste at the end of my driveway.

But things are different now.

My daughters and I had just finished baking several types of valentine treats for their beloved teachers, friends, and family. The girls were sitting at the kitchen table with puffy heart stickers and neon-colored markers, carefully decorating cards to accompany the goodies. That is when I made my announcement.

"I have been thinking about our trash collectors. How often do you think there is a surprise waiting for them next to the trash can?"

Without hesitation, Natalie said, "Never," and carefully placed the top on the bright pink marker and stared at me. She knew something was coming.

I continued explaining my thoughts to my attentive and ever-willing Hands Free assistants. "Sometimes I wonder what those hardworking people go home to at the end of the day. I wonder if they have little kids who hug them. I wonder how often they come home knowing that people are thankful they took their trash away."

I pointed to the craft supplies scattered about the table and further elaborated. "Maybe it's been a long time since these workers saw a colorful package sitting next to a trash receptacle. Maybe they *never* have had a treat waiting for them."

I noticed my children were soaking in every detail I offered of a life so unfamiliar to their own. I could tell they yearned to know more. "What if they saw your beautifully decorated bags and homemade cookies? Don't you think they would smile and feel appreciated?"

The girls nodded vigorously. That's when I leaned in and got to the point.

"It is easy to remember to appreciate the people who are our friends and loved ones. It's hard to remember the other people, but they are just as important. We should remember them too." And then I posed one final thought. "Just imagine how happy you could make someone."

The girls immediately sprang into action. While grabbing cards and markers, ideas began to flow. Natalie suggested that along with the baked goods, the trash collectors would need "energy." She decided we should bag healthy trail mix to provide them with fuel to lift heavy trash containers. She distinctly pointed out that the mix must not contain candy. (And all along I thought I had been talking to myself when I said sugar does not give you energy.)

Avery was enthusiastic about decorating the gift bags. She spent an hour using five Sharpies, an entire bottle of glitter glue, and an assortment of puffy stickers to create an artistic display. When completely dry, it appeared that the bag could withstand an unexpected monsoon while waiting curbside.

I was amazed and delighted. The kids were putting as much time, thought, care, and effort into the gifts for people they did *not* know as they did for the people they *did* know. Just the thought of surprising someone who did not get many surprises inspired my daughters in ways I had not imagined.

On the morning of trash pickup, each girl carried her bag out to the curb. Once the brightly colored bags were positioned next to the contrasting dingy canister, the girls stood back in admiration and excitement.

A little while later, we were upstairs getting ready for school when we heard the roar of the garbage truck. The girls ran to the window and had a perfect aerial view of the happy little scene.

We saw a man, who normally works at lightning speed to

empty canisters and hop back on the truck, actually pause when he saw the gifts.

It appeared that we caught him off guard.

It appeared that a decorated gift bag was the last thing he expected to find next to a trash can.

It appeared that he was not convinced these bags were for him.

Then it appeared that although there was hesitation, he finally accepted that these gifts really were for him.

It appeared that it was just what he needed on an unusually cold and unlikely snow day in the South.

But I must admit, what touched me even more deeply than the awestruck look on the man's face were the expressions of the little people who had created this moment. Peering out the window with wide smiles were two children who realized that despite having small hands, they held great power. By placing a token of love outside the usual circle of family and friends, they proved that beauty and kindness can be found in the dingiest of places. And when it is, the world as we know it becomes a little bit brighter and a little more hopeful.

 ## HANDS FREE WEEKLY INTENTION

Impact a Service Person's Life with Kindness

One thing that was important to me even while I was living distracted was to teach my children how to engage in acts of kindness. Therefore, I tried to involve them in giving activities from an early age. If they could hold a spoon or a crayon, they helped me bring happiness to others. As we baked muffins for neighbors or made get-well cards for ill relatives, I always took the time to explain why we were doing it and how it would make that person feel to receive such a gift. It wasn't long before my children started making cards on their own for sick classmates or suggesting we bake treats for a beloved teacher or family member. My children began recognizing people who needed cheering up or appreciation even when I failed to notice.

To be honest, it would have been much easier, less messy, and more efficient if I had not involved my children in these gift-giving practices. But by sharing the experience with them, it cultivated a desire in their hearts to bring joy to the lives of others. Raising kind and generous children has always been something that really matters to me, so any inconveniences that their involvement added were of little significance.

This week, come together as a family to create a token of appreciation for someone who provides a service for you. It does not have to be Valentine's Day to leave unexpected gifts for those who are seldom thanked. In fact, gifts that come at unexpected times from unexpected sources often mean the most!

Think about the underappreciated, often forgotten people in your life. Perhaps the mail carrier, school secretary, bank teller, or your favorite cashier could use a little pick-me-up. It doesn't have to be an extravagant gesture. Nor does it have to be expensive or require a lot of time. Simply express appreciation in a way that is comfortable and fitting for you. Someone will undoubtedly be touched by your gesture.

IT ONLY TAKES ONE MOMENT

As we prepared for a house full of holiday guests, Natalie sat in the middle of the kitchen floor, gift-wrapping used books and small toiletry items. She placed them into a large blue sack and announced that she wanted to pass out these gifts to homeless people in the morning.

My husband and I suggested taking the gifts to a nearby facility for teenage mothers rather than navigate the downtown area of our city. But Natalie quickly rejected this idea, confidently stating, "No, I really want to pass out these gifts and money to people on the streets."

My husband and I exchanged glances, neither of us knowing exactly how to handle our child's lofty ambition. We assured her we would think about what to do with the gifts and let her know the next day.

A good night's sleep did nothing to lessen Natalie's persistence. At eight o'clock in the morning she was asking when we were leaving and how we should distribute the gifts. She had even thought to decorate envelopes in which cash could be placed.

I must admit, I was preoccupied with selfish thoughts about the hundred things I had to do around the house to prepare for our company that was due to arrive in a few hours. I also planned to take a morning run and had a few last-minute gifts to wrap. But when I looked at her with that huge bag slung over her shoulder, ready to spread peace and love with her two small hands, my heart felt an undeniable tug. I realized this was a critical moment to let go of distraction and grasp what really mattered.

As our family drove to the ATM in a low-income area of our city, we still hadn't decided exactly how we were going to distribute the gifts. The plan at the moment was simply to look out the window and stop when we saw someone we thought might be in need.

As our car pulled away from the bank, I could see in the distance an odd situation in the parking lot of a gas station. An entire family stood outside their dilapidated vehicle, their distressed postures and rapid pacing around their car indicated something was terribly wrong. I grabbed my husband's arm and said, "Drive over there."

The line of traffic between the gas station and our car was thick. As we waited for the opportunity to cross the street, I saw the woman go inside the gas station.

I quickly stuffed a wad of cash into one of my child's cheerily decorated envelopes and told Natalie to grab one of her wrapped gifts. I informed her that we were going to give it to the woman inside the gas station.

When we walked in, the petite woman stood before the gas station ATM with her head slumped down, her bony hands stretching her sweater tightly around her shivering body. It was apparent she had been unsuccessful at getting any money out.

I walked up to her and said, "We can see you are having some difficulty today and wanted to give you this."

With a look of utter disbelief, the woman slowly opened the unsealed envelope. When she saw the contents, she covered her gaping mouth with a trembling hand. Tears began streaming down her beautiful, unblemished skin.

When I asked if there was anything else we could do to help, she said, "You have already done more than you know . . . more than you know."

As I reached to embrace her with every fiber of strength and hope I possessed, I saw Natalie peering up at us with the most wondrous look on her face. It appeared as though she was seeing something truly miraculous for the very first time.

I could read my child's mind. I wanted to say, "Yes, my sweet child, it's this easy. It is this easy to change a person's entire day . . . maybe even a person's entire life."

After leaving the gas station, we drove aimlessly around the city. Seventeen more opportunities to extend hope and love presented themselves in a matter of one hour. Each response was different, but the significance of the moment was evident in the gratitude etched across each recipient's face.

As my family drove home in joyful silence, I knew not one of us would forget this remarkable day. I was so grateful that a persistent little girl with a generous spirit had listened to the callings of her heart. And I was beyond grateful that I had pushed away my distractions long enough to listen to my own. Suddenly I was reminded why I must continue my journey to live Hands Free.

Because all it takes is *one* moment.

That moment when you choose to push aside your to-do list, turn off the phone, shut down the computer . . .

That moment when you admit it won't kill you if you skip a workout . . .

That moment you laugh and remind yourself that friends and family do not care about dirty floors or a perfectly decorated home ...

That moment you acknowledge that time should not be wasted worrying about achieving perfection that does not exist ...

That moment you choose to let go of what distracts you from what really matters is the moment your eyes are opened to the many opportunities you have to reach outside yourself and touch a life.

Being Hands Free is not about getting it "right" all the time; we're human after all and daily distractions are abundant. But every time I listen to the callings of my heart, I *do* get it right.

Because when you find yourself in the right place at the right time, looking into the eyes of a person who almost seemed to be waiting for you, everything else seems insignificant in that one moment.

One moment is all it takes to change a life.

 ## HANDS FREE WEEKLY INTENTION

Impact a Stranger's Life with Kindness

When I was in my distracted state, my purpose for giving was either to check something off the list, to receive gratitude, or to earn public accolades. That all changed the day my children left Easter baskets for the trash collectors. The Valentine's Day bags had been such a hit that my daughters were encouraged to leave Easter treats a few months later. When they arrived home from school that day, they hopped out of the car and searched all around the empty canisters. I thought they were looking for a gift in return for the Easter baskets.

When my child called out, "Yep, they got 'em! I bet our trash guys were happy!" I realized how selfish my thoughts were. The children were happy simply because their gifts had been received. That is how

I wanted to live ... expressing love and kindness to those around me without expecting anything in return ... offering to help someone without expecting a reciprocated favor or a thank-you note ... thinking of others because it is the right thing to do ... blessing others as we have been so richly blessed by God ... and because exhibiting kindness toward another person without a hidden agenda is a generous and content way to live.

Once that notion of heartfelt giving was realized, my children and I began looking for ways to help people we didn't know. Sometimes this meant not seeing the results of our actions. Sometimes this meant trusting the right person would receive what was given. Sometimes this meant giving something of value even if we couldn't control what the recipient did with it. Hands Free gift-giving meant letting go of what we couldn't control to grasp what really mattered and letting God meet someone else's needs through our willing hands.

This week, choose to impact a stranger's life with kindness.

Every day, there are opportunities to be guardian angels for people in need. By calling your child's school or a local church or merely opening your eyes while traveling in the town in which you live, you can provide a helping hand. Just be on the lookout for an opportunity to touch a life ...

She might be standing at the bus stop in worn-out shoes.

He might be sitting on the corner of Delaware and Sixteenth with despair in his eyes.

She might be waiting in line behind you at the grocery store wondering if ten dollars will cover the diapers and milk.

He might be seated in the desk next to your child hoping his mom can afford the five-dollar field-trip fee.

Simply let go of distraction for one moment. In that moment, you have the power to make a significant connection with another human being. You have the opportunity to be in the right place at the right time. Simply open your eyes and hands to grasp it.

The King will reply, "Truly I tell you, whatever you did for one of the least of these brothers and sisters of mine, you did for me."
(Matthew 25:40)

TO FIX WHAT IS BROKEN

I had been searching for a tangible way to introduce the concept of giving to my children when a brochure literally landed right in my lap one Sunday morning at church. The pamphlet showed a picture of an ordinary shoebox being packed with school supplies, hygiene items, toys, socks, and other small items. The box would travel to a child living in poverty. It would provide much-needed provisions, in addition to hope and love.

It was exactly the project I had been looking for.

Before I presented the shoebox project to my children, I wanted to know specifics about the recipients of the boxes. Late one night I did some online research using the phrase "stories of children living in poverty." Little did I know that what I was about to see would stir a passion in my heart that would forever change my family's life.

In darkened solitude, I sat in front of my computer, clicking the mouse as if it were a never-ending Rolodex of forsaken children with desperation in their eyes.

The more I clicked, the more hopeless their eyes became. I could have clicked until dawn; it was apparent that such devastation had no end. But then I saw it, and I knew I had come to my end ... or shall I say, my beginning. I stopped at the image of one child and needed to see no more.

He was a small boy about two or three years old in a tattered blue shirt, wearing no pants. His beautiful dark skin was caked in dried mud. In his hands he clutched his one and only toy. It was a rusted tricycle that was missing its tires, but he held it like it was his prized possession. I was swallowed up into dark eyes that reflected unspeakable pain and suffering. My shoulders shook as I sobbed. The image of this child jumped from the computer screen straight into my heart.

Although I knew a random recipient would receive our shoebox gift, I also knew with certainty that we must fill a shoebox for him, the boy with the broken bike.

What I wouldn't do to fix his brokenness.

The next day, I showed the photo to Natalie, who was five years old at the time. I pointed to the bike and explained that this was his only toy, yet he cherished it because it was all he had. I then proceeded to tell her all the other details I had learned about him in very basic terms. I told her that his brother's only toy was a tin can, and sometimes he got cut while playing with it. I told her of the corn mush he felt lucky to eat once a day. When food was not available, his mother made "cookies" out of dirt so their bellies would not feel empty. I showed her the yellow water he drank, that his mother had to walk for hours to acquire. I defined the word *contaminated* by explaining that he drank water in which people and animals bathe and go to the bathroom. I showed her pictures of a shack that could be his house where there is no bed, no warmth, no light, and no safety.

Finally, I showed her the shoebox. I said, "This box is empty right now, but you can fill it with things the little boy needs, and some very special people will make sure it gets to him."

The devastated expression on her face instantly brightened by this notion. "I can help him, Mama," she announced as she ran off smiling.

In less than five minutes she had collected a new toothbrush, a bar of soap, pencils, a small notebook, a new pair of socks, a stuffed animal, and her favorite candy. She showed me each item proudly. My child could not grasp the magnitude of poverty, but she easily understood the simple fact that the things this boy needed were things that she possessed.

Later that day, Natalie began talking about the boy with the broken bike while she ate her wholesome dinner. His image and his story had stuck with her. He was now a part of her mind and her heart. It was then I knew with certainty that I must show more children his image and show them a simple, yet powerful way they can impact the world. I didn't know how this would be possible, so I prayed that God would make it clear to me.

That night I had the most vivid dream. There was a huge

gathering where groups of children were being taught by adults. And of course, there were shoeboxes, stacks and stacks of them in every corner of the huge room.

I woke up with a start, my mind and heart clear on what I must do.

I went to my pastor and explained my idea for a community gathering where I would teach the young attendees what life is like for children living in poverty. By seeing that many of the basic items the children needed are in our homes, I felt the attendees could use their own two hands to do something good for someone else. I felt God's presence every step of the way, assuring me he would work out the details.

Fast-forward five years ...

I have been honored to share stories and images of children in poverty with hundreds of young people since 2009. Although I create a new PowerPoint presentation each year, the image of the boy with the broken bike is one constant. And the reaction is always the same.

Bewilderment.

Shock.

Disbelief.

Sorrow.

When I lift the lid of the shoebox and tell the children of the emptiness happening in the lives of those in desperate situations, I see eyes opening; I see hearts opening; I see hands opening.

Before I even get to the part about packing a shoebox I ask, "Why do you think I am telling you about such sad lives and showing you pictures of heartbroken children?"

The hands fly up because they know ... they know.

With the conviction of an experienced child advocate, there is always one child who says, "Because we *need* to do something to help these kids."

Oh yes, no matter how young, someone gets it right every single time.

The children then see how an empty shoebox can be transformed into a gift that includes much more than hygiene items, school supplies, toys, and candy. The box holds the healing light of hope for a broken soul, and their hands have the power to create that light.

The children then go home and excitedly begin filling their shoeboxes with needed items, just as my daughter did.

Stories like this one are common in the days following my presentation on poverty:

> My seven-year-old son came to me while wrapping the shoeboxes and said, "I've decided I'm going to put all my allowance savings into the shoebox."
>
> I was astounded. He had been saving a very long time for something he really wanted. I tried to convince him that I would purchase the gifts to go in the box, but he was adamant.
>
> "I don't want to use it to buy anything," he said, "I just want to put it in there with the other gifts."
>
> My eyes welled up with tears, and his eyes welled up with tears. It is just one of those moments I will remember for a long time. And so will my son.
>
> *Jennifer and Josh*

I've opened over a thousand shoeboxes that have been filled by a child. There is always evidence that other children, like Josh, decided to place their "life savings" in the shoebox as well. And without fail, I always find a box that contains tools. Someone always packs tools, hoping their box will be given to the boy with the broken bike.

What we wouldn't do to fix his brokenness.

Unfortunately, I can't tell you if a shoebox gift has ever reached that precious boy. But I can tell you with certainty that someone was reached. A year after we sent our first shoebox, we received a letter. I knew immediately upon opening the mailbox that we were about to be given a remarkable gift. I ran into the house yelling for Natalie. She met me in the entryway looking puzzled about the tears streaming down my face.

"Someone received our shoebox!" I cried.

At the time, my daughter did not yet understand how rare it

was to receive a response from a shoebox recipient. Most do not have the means to purchase a stamp, write a letter, or access a post office. My hands shook as I opened it. Then I saw his face, a beautiful little boy standing next to his big sister—both so delighted by the gifts we had packed inside a simple shoebox. The boy's father had written to thank us for sending the gift to their family at a time when it was most needed. Our shoebox containing the light of hope and love reached a family whose last name was "Sunny."

Coincidence? I think not.

My daughter and I knew that letter was a divine sign to keep spreading the light of hope in the world and to show others how to join us.

We have corresponded with the Sunny family over the past several years. After sending care packages to them, we receive pictures of their family sharing the treats with other children in their village.

Each time we receive pictures from their village, I find myself studying every face ... looking for *him*.

My rational mind knows I will not see the boy with the broken bike, but my heart still searches for him. I am confident one day he will be reached. He will be reached with the light of hope that radiates through the smallest of hands.

For these are the hands that hold the power to fix all that is broken.

 ## HANDS FREE WEEKLY INTENTION

Impact the World with Kindness

What started out as a personal desire to educate young minds about poverty through an Operation Christmas Child shoebox has turned into an annual family endeavor. As my children have grown, so has their involvement in all aspects related to the project. Each year, I watch in amazement as they fill more and more shoeboxes on their own. Being a part of this effort has expanded my children's interests into other global issues, like sponsoring a child through Compassion International and contributing to Water for Life.

Somewhere along the line, extending kindness has turned into a habit, a natural reaction, and a daily practice for our family. No atrocity seems too big, no sufferer seems too far. My children have learned that even a tiny ripple of hope created by their small hands is enough to make a difference.

Take notice in your community. Keep your eyes open as you go through town. What suffering do you see? What brokenness is apparent that a little love and compassion might heal? Identify a need and share it with a child in age-appropriate terms. Give small hands a chance to rise to the occasion. You will be astounded by what they can do.

Earth's Kids *www.earthskids.com* is a great resource that provides the information, links, and the tools to help kids make a difference in their community and the world. There are a variety of issues listed with resources provided for each one:

- saving the environment
- ending world hunger
- working for world peace
- ending poverty
- providing service in your community

Not only is working together on a worthy cause a great way to connect and spend time with children, but it teaches lifelong skills and important values that contribute to a meaningful and gratitude-filled life.

HANDS FREE REFLECTION

Compassion
The Light of Human Connection

It is in the children's faces and words when they are listened to and loved.

It is in the lost, the broken, and the hopeless when someone looks them in the eye and regards them as human beings.

It is in the elderly, in their deep facial lines, their precious memories, and that twinkle in the eye when treated with respect and kindness.

It is in the heart of a toddler when new shoes are placed on feet that have never known such comfort.

It is in a man's grateful smile when his customer presents him with a cold bottled water as he grooms the landscape.

It is in a waitress's tearful eyes when she is given a generous tip when it is needed most.

It is in a wrapped shoebox making its way from one continent to another.

It is in a lovingly decorated bag sitting on top of a trash can.

It is in homemade cookies brought to the fire station.

It is in our hands.

It is in our hearts.

It is in our power.

The light of human connection—it is right at our fingertips, right in our line of vision, but it is so often untouched and unseen beneath the veil of distractions, the hurry, the to-do lists, and the futile attempts at perfection.

But the light is there, and it is ours for the taking when we allow our soul to merge with another.

What is the point in being alive if you fail to see the light?

See it today.

See it in a child.

> See it in a loved one.
> See it in a friend, a service person, or a stranger.
> And once you see it, let that marvelous light spill across your heart
> and bring what really matters clearly into focus.

REFLECTION QUESTIONS

Do you ever experience the callings of the heart when you see someone in need? How do you respond? What specific distractions and/or reservations prevent you from responding? Describe a time when you acted on an urge to help someone. What was the outcome?

How involved are your children in expressing appreciation to others or helping people in need? Name a few ways you could encourage your children to perform acts of kindness and express appreciation toward others who touch their lives.

We are often bombarded with requests to give of our time, talents, and/or money when it comes to charitable causes. How might your family decide what causes or missions are most important to you? Name a few specific ways you could support the causes you hold dear.

Chapter 12

REMEMBER LIFE IS PRECIOUS

Gratefulness

Normal day, let me be aware of the treasure you are.
Let me learn from you, love you, bless you before you depart.
Let me not pass you by in quest of some rare and perfect
tomorrow.

Mary Jean Irion

IT MIGHT SOUND ODD, but I don't regret the two years of my highly distracted life. Those years showed me what I *didn't* want my life to look like. Through each one of the steps in my Hands Free journey, I developed a clear vision of what I *did* want my life to look like.

By the time I reached this final step in the journey, there was no question about how I wanted to spend my precious time on earth. There was no question what kind of childhood I wanted my children to remember as adults. There was no question that the most important things in life are not "things." It was time to seal my commitment to the beautiful Hands Free practice that, by the grace of God, had become my way of life.

This final step was a time of reflection. It allowed me to appreciate the progress I had made and recognize how far I had come. Taking this step offered me a chance to marvel at all the divine signs I had encountered. Each providential confirmation fueled and strengthened my pursuit of a present and gratitude-filled life. From where I stood, twelve steps into the journey, a Hands Free life was the only life I ever wanted to know. It was the only way I wanted to live out my remaining days here on earth.

This chapter includes stories about the significant experiences that confirmed I was on the right path. Each experience cultivated gratitude for the blessings of life by weighing it against life's fragility. As you read each story, may you be reminded of the preciousness of life. As you reflect on your own journey, may you be encouraged to make whatever changes you need to make in your daily habits to solidify your commitment to living Hands Free.

SIGNS OF LIFE

From a very young age, Natalie has had a passion for teaching small children. At age seven, this passion spurred her to create a summer school in the playroom of our home for four soon-to-be kindergarteners. While teaching and lesson-planning were her strengths, organization and cleanliness were not. In fact, the week before students were due to arrive, Natalie found her "classroom" in a bit of a disaster.

Where there once were organized drawers of school supplies, there were now crowded bins packed with *randomness*. (Need an extra sock, anyone?)

Where there once was a clean desk with tidy stacks of lesson plans, there was now an unidentifiable object buried under two feet of *randomness*.

Where there once were containers of sharpened pencils and crayons sorted by color, there were now tubs of miscellaneous *randomness*.

In the midst of this wall-to-wall *randomness* stood my daughter, with hopeful brown eyes, asking *me* if I would help her get things organized.

I had to give her credit for coming to the right place. Despite my new Hands Free status, the control freak inside me could be summoned at any time. My daughter knew I still possessed the ability to seize any disorganized area and create harmonious order within a record amount of time.

The mere thought of her happy face while teaching her small students motivated me to help. But with every drawer that exploded when opened, my impatience grew. My inner drill sergeant immediately came to life, quickly dismissing Hands Free Rachel who was utterly useless in situations like these. I soon heard myself firing off directives to the teacher-in-training who looked downright appalled that she had actually enticed The Organization Monster to come out.

After one hour, a handful of my most exasperated sighs, and two completely overextended trash bags, we restored order to the area. As I dragged an enormous bag to the recycling bin, I quickly assessed the effort of my child, who was paper-clipping math sheets as instructed. Although my inner drill sergeant does not stop for anything (including thirst, hunger, or bodily injury), my feet became cemented when a small, colorful sign caught my eye. The sign was clipped to a basket of handmade word tiles. As I bent over to read the sign, my daughter enthusiastically explained, "That's the Language Arts Center. I made it myself. Do you like it, Mama?"

I swallowed the lump in my throat. While I had been huffing and puffing in drill sergeant tunnel vision mode, what else had I missed?

As I surveyed the room, this time looking for flowers instead of weeds, my eyes filled with tears when I saw all the things I missed due to my distractedness ...

- folders for each of her four students
- a library stocked with colorful children's books sorted by reading level
- an "About the Teacher" parent brochure

- four sets of take-home books
- a parent letter about developing the love of reading in a child
- an "Art Room Rules" pamphlet

Then came the big one—the biggest oversight of all.

Four clean desks, each graced with a beautifully colored nameplate and a brand new pencil, sat waiting for the precious children who would soon sit in them.

It appeared that while drawers had become disorganized and surfaces had collected piles, something else had been taking place—something far more important than being tidy: living ... creating ... and making dreams come true.

In the process of using her God-given talents and passions, my daughter created something of lasting value. And when I slowed down long enough to take it all in, I saw there had been some *real* living going on.

I saw signs of life.

After expressing gratitude to me for helping, Natalie sat down at her desk and began filling out her lesson-plan book. I kissed the top of her head and said, "I love to watch you be a teacher. And I'm sorry I went a little crazy at the beginning of our cleaning session."

I walked downstairs grinning to myself about how excited she and the students would be on that first day of school. But as soon as I entered my bedroom, my smile rapidly dissipated. My jaw dropped. Go ahead—take one guess as to what I saw.

Pile after pile after pile ...

Every corner of my bedroom held a pile. Granted, I could tell you what each stack represented and could find anything I needed in less than sixty seconds. But make no mistake, there was a vertical eyesore inhabiting every corner of the room. I was surrounded by hundreds of notes, journals filled to the brim, and scraps of paper scrawled with writing ideas that came to me while standing in line at the grocery store.

It didn't used to be this way, you know.

During my highly distracted years, things were in order—even if it meant staying up until two o'clock in the morning to do it. I didn't sit on the couch for close to two years because there was always something to be picked up, organized, folded, or put away. (God forbid someone would stop by and see people actually lived in my house.) If we were having weekend guests, I organized all the kitchen drawers for fear someone might open one.

And this last part, although difficult to admit now, illustrates how misconstrued my thoughts were about what was important. Each day before I left the house, I reminded myself that if I were in a car accident, someone might come to the house to gather clothes for the funeral. That dismal thought motivated me to make my bed and clean off the kitchen counters. Seriously? I just told myself I may only have a couple hours to live and I'm thinking about housekeeping!

Talk about tragic.

Oh yes, for two distracted years, my house was always tidy and the bedroom corners were void of piles.

But there were no Hands Free stories, words, or experiences. There were no messages that inspired people to let go of distraction and connect to what matters. There was no legacy of my time here on earth.

To put it bluntly, there was no Hands Free Mama. She did not exist—not even in my wildest dreams.

Oh yes, my corners were empty. And so was I.

As I thought about my daughter, who was passionately writing lessons in her plan book, I picked up my white binder—the one that contained my very first experiences of living Hands Free. It was teetering proudly on the top of pile number three like the prized cherry on a sundae.

I held the binder to my chest and acknowledged this wasn't just a collection of papers. It was my heart, soul, blood, sweat, and tears—a loving chronicle of precious memories made with my children and my spouse that had sparked my journey to live Hands Free.

That's when it hit me. Some things in life are incongruent. There are just some things you simply cannot grasp if you're holding on to something else. *To grasp what matters, you must let go of what doesn't!*

Whether I realized it or not, I had let go of the need for clean corners, the preoccupation with how things look to outsiders, and the pressure to "do it all" so I could live the life I am meant to live. Perhaps it was time I allowed my children that same reprieve. Because when my daughter is grown and asks me what she was like as a child, there will be no mention of her messy room or her lack of organization. I will tell her she taught kindergarten to four small children who came to love, admire, and aspire to be just like her. I will tell her that at the mere age of seven, she was creating a lasting legacy.

And if my life should come to a tragic end and a friend must fetch clothes for my funeral, something tells me she will gasp when she enters my bedroom—but not because she sees an unsightly mess. She will gasp because decorating every corner of my room will be tiny pieces of me scribbled on paper after paper.

Signs of life.

And I imagine my friend will bend down and pick one up. She will read my words and feel my presence. As tears quietly stream down her face, my friend will be grateful I spent the precious years of my life *living* Hands Free instead of dying to keep the corners clean.

HANDS FREE WEEKLY INTENTION

Be a Living Hands Free Example

What do you do when you want to live Hands Free but your spouse or children are tied to their distractions? This may seem like an uphill battle, but a relationship with the people you love is worth the fight.

This week, encourage your loved ones to engage in Hands Free practices by modeling desired behaviors. Here are some suggestions that can help transform a tech-obsessed family into a Hands Free family.

Consistently invite your family members to engage in activities that do not involve electronic devices or technology, such as:

- cooking
- sewing
- board games
- nature walks/hikes
- bike rides
- arts and crafts, painting, or woodworking projects
- science experiments
- sporting events

You know the hobbies your family members enjoy, so suggest activities that would be of interest to them. If necessary, you may need to tell, rather than ask, your loved ones to put away the devices and engage as a family. I have discovered that even if my children are resistant to the idea at first, they almost always end up enjoying the experience and don't want it to end. The whole family walks away from this shared time feeling happier and more relaxed than if we had remained tied to our individual distractions. With each successful family adventure, the willingness to let go of distraction comes more readily.

Be an example of what it means to live presently, and continually verbalize the benefits you receive from living Hands Free.

- Point out beautiful things you see in nature while driving that you would have missed if you were using the phone.
- Announce to the family that you are not taking your device into the restaurant (or any establishment or event) so that you can connect to the people around you.
- Note how enjoyable it is to watch your children engage in extracurricular activities or sporting events when your phone is put away.

- Share your observations about the improvements you've noticed in your relationships since changing phone habits at home or in the car.

Reinforce desired behavior. Even if your family member attempts small efforts to let go of distraction, be sure to let him or her know you noticed. Thank your loved ones for spending time as a family without the device present. Let your loved ones know how much it means to you that they are investing time, love, and attention into your relationship.

As you begin to live more presently, you will become happier and more content. Whether your family chooses to join you on the Hands Free journey or not, you will be a living reminder that the best moments in life happen when we turn off the phone and other electronic devices. That is a legacy that could impact not only your children's lives but also their children's lives, as well.

AN OPEN LETTER TO TIME

Dear Time,

I recently attended my daughter's end-of-the-year program that was held in her kindergarten classroom. As she stood in the front of the room beaming at me with her crinkly-eyed smile, I was overcome by the most unsettling feeling. I could have sworn I was sitting in that same pint-sized chair watching her older sister sing the same adorable medley of tunes just yesterday. Yesterday.

But that was three years ago.

Time, you seem to get away from me.

So tonight I went upstairs to watch my children sleep. I'll be honest, I hadn't done that in a while. As I opened the door to my younger child's room, I took a deep breath. I had a feeling this was going to hurt. But nothing could have prepared me for what I was about to experience.

As my eyes adjusted to the darkened room, the sight of my

sleeping "baby" in her bed startled me. When did her legs make such a long, vertical lump—coming alarmingly close to the end of the bed?

I quietly stepped closer and peered at her peacefully clasped hands. When did her knuckles lose their precious chubby indentations? Where there used to be pillows of scrumptious skin, I could now see bony little knobs.

No, no, no! I quickly covered my mouth so that my inevitable sob would not slip out and wake her. *Time, you seem to get away from me.*

Although my heart didn't want to go there, my eyes tentatively came to rest on her lovely face. Somewhere in the past few months, the perfectly round shape of her head had begun to elongate into an adult-like oval. That is when I lost it.

Curse you, Time!

Curse you!

Curse you!

Tonight I just wanted to grab you, Time. Tackle you. Pin you down and stop you from going forward at lightning pace.

Believe me, I know. I can see you rolling your eyes. I know what you're thinking. I haven't respected you like I should ... always criticizing you ... ordering you to hurry up ... whining when I have to wait—even if it's just for a few minutes.

Rarely do I simply enjoy you.

Rarely am I satisfied with you.

Rarely, if ever, do I cherish and appreciate you.

You are so right.

But here's the problem, Time. I'm afraid you're going to run out on me, and I've got things to do. You're probably thinking I just want more time to complete my never-ending to-do list, more time to complete unimportant tasks that won't matter twenty years from now. Because that is how I lived for so long.

But thing are different now—so different. You see, my eyes have been opened. And for the first time in my life, I can see what is truly important.

When I got down on my knees and leaned close enough to feel my child's warm, rhythmic breath on my face tonight, the words came. I was finally able to articulate what I need more time to do. So now, Time, I throw myself at your mercy and ask you to hear my plea ...

There's a spot on her face I have yet to kiss.

There's a freckle on her nose I have yet to count.

There's a place on her back I have yet to scratch.

There's a scent in her hair I have yet to inhale.

There's a place on her belly I have yet to rub.

There's a laugh in her chest I have yet to hear.

There's a joyful expression on her face I have yet to see.

There's a dream in her heart I have yet to believe.

There's a song in her throat I have yet to hear.

There's a word of love I have yet to speak.

There's an apology I have yet to offer.

There's an embrace I have yet to provide.

And so I need more time.

For I can't bear to let a spot go unkissed, a word go unsaid, or a strand of hair go untouched.

Not in this lifetime.

Not in her lifetime.

With each passing day I accomplish so much, yet when it comes to the things that really matter, I accomplish so little.

But not today.

Time,

today I will not waste you.

Time,

today I will not take you for granted.

Time,

today I will make the most of every second you have to offer.

Time,

today I will be thankful.

Thankful you have not run out on me.

Thankful I still have time to kiss her face, tickle her belly, and count her freckles.

Today I will be thankful for Time.

Because you haven't run out on me.

Not yet, anyway.

Because I know full well that you can.

And you have

for some precious souls who thought they would have time tomorrow

to kiss, to laugh, to hug, to dance, to run, to play,

to live.

But time ran out.

So today I will be thankful for the Time I have.

And I will use it for good.

Sincerely,

Rachel, a woman whose eyes have been opened to see the preciousness of Time

 ## HANDS FREE WEEKLY INTENTION

Use Time for Good

All day long, you have choices about how you spend your limited time and resources. When you begin to develop a Hands Free mentality, you become more mindful of these choices. You continually evaluate how the choices you make impact your life, your current relationships, as well as your future relationships. Having a Hands Free mentality means you make choices that bring you *closer* to the people you love, rather than separate or strain your relationships.

If you haven't already begun doing so, make it a habit to consider your options when you recognize a spontaneous opportunity to grasp what really matters.

Ask yourself:

- Could this (phone call, work assignment, Facebook status update) be done later?

- Could this (laundry folding, car washing, house cleaning, dinner preparation) be done as a family?
- Could I think of a more beneficial way to wait for the movie, sporting event, or concert to start instead of looking at my phone?
- Could I set aside my inhibitions and step out of my comfort zone to enjoy the moment at hand with my family?
- Could I do what I want to do later and engage in this activity with my child or spouse now?

Sometimes the answer will be no. That is life. As adults, sometimes we must do what we need to do. But other times you will find yourself saying, "Right now, I see an opportunity to connect with my loved one, and that is the most important thing I can do right now." Choosing connection over distraction offers a chance to nurture your most sacred relationships — now and in the future. I cannot think of a better use of your precious time, can you?

I HAVE A DISEASE

It may seem odd to end the book with a confession, but this is how the whole journey got started, so this, too, is how it shall end.

- I've used the phrase "hurry up" more times in one day than a person should use in a lifetime.
- I came frighteningly close to convincing myself that checking email messages at stoplights was not a dangerous practice.
- There have been occasions when I had to type my to-do list because it was so long.
- I've been known to check my phone just because I walked by it.
- I repeatedly succumbed to the pressure to say yes to volunteer duties when I knew they would suck life out of me.
- I've spent embarrassing amounts of time reading frivolous

information on the Internet when I could have been talking to my children or spouse.

- There were times I chose to ruin a perfectly beautiful moment because I felt less than perfect in some way.
- My ability to find one more thing to do before I sit down has resulted in collapsing from exhaustion.
- I've missed a lot of priceless moments, and I will never get them back.

You see, I have a disease. It's called The Disease of Distraction. Perhaps some of these symptoms sound familiar. Maybe you can even think of a few debilitating symptoms of your own. I don't know what type of distraction disease you have or the severity of it.

But if you own a phone,

or a television,

or a computer,

or a tablet ...

If you find yourself constantly checking, updating, posting, texting, recording, watching, commenting, uploading, downloading, surfing, or browsing ...

If you live in the twenty-first century,

Then you may be affected by this disease.

If you find yourself reaching for your phone instead of talking or playing with your kids,

If your calendar is filled with a constant flurry of activity,

If you feel like you never slow down,

If you get through the day and realize that you haven't made eye contact or real conversation with someone you love,

Then you may be affected by the disease.

If you can't rest until the mess is cleaned up,

The dishes are put away,

The laundry is folded,

If you find yourself constantly saying "just a minute" to the ones who call for you,

Then there's a good chance you might be affected by this disease.

If you allow yourself to be preoccupied over the details of the perfect meal,
The perfect table setting,
The perfect house,
The perfect decor,
The perfect outfit,
And the perfect body in its perfect size,
Then you might be affected.

If you constantly feel your attention being averted from what really matters to the insignificant and meaningless details of your life, then you might be familiar with The Disease of Distraction. It grips you so tightly that it prevents you from living in the present moment. It blocks your view of the precious gifts that are right in front of your face. It causes you to feel stressed, anxious, and empty instead of grateful, calm, and content.

But wait! I urge you not to accept that this is *just the way it's going to be.*
There's a cure.

And it works every time you need to be shaken, pulled back in, and slapped in the face to see what truly matters.
It's simple.
It's so very simple.

THE CURE FOR THE DISEASE OF DISTRACTION

Look at your child's eyelashes and marvel at their perfect symmetry.
They will look different a year from now.

Reach for his hand and remember how it feels in your own.
It will be bigger a year from now.

Listen to her sing "You Are My Sunshine." Close your eyes and memorize her voice.
It will not sound so childlike a year from now.

Watch her sleep as she awaits a visit from the tooth fairy.
She will believe a little less in magical things a year from now.

Let him help in the kitchen. Taste much and laugh often.
You might find he is no longer your shadow a year from now.

Teach her something she's been asking to learn. Encourage and
guide her.
She might be able to do it by herself a year from now.

Offer to play tag in the yard. Watch him delight as you chase him.
You might not be able to keep up a year from now.

Sit with him as he eats his cereal. Listen to his philosophy of life.
He may not have as much to share a year from now.

Tell her favorite story for the millionth time as she nestles in
the crook of your arm.
She may not fit so perfectly a year from now.
Stare at his face. See yourself in the amazing individual before you.
You may see a little less of yourself in him a year from now.

It is in moments like these that time stops, the insignificant
falls away. The only thing that matters is the present moment and
the precious human being in your company.

And the reason I write these words with grateful tears streaming down my face is because I know with certainty this is The
Cure for Distraction. This consuming disease robbed me of two
years of *living*—the laughing, playing, memory-making parts of
life … the parts of life that really matter.

By the grace of God, I have been in recovery since July 2010.

I have seen the light.

I didn't find it by looking at the screen of my computer. I didn't
find it in thousands of emails, text messages, or extracurricular
commitments. I didn't find it in the smallest size clothing I ever
wore. I found it here, in my hands, when I let go of distraction
and connected with the people I love. That is when I was set free
from the chains of distraction. That is when I truly began living.

So today, go for the cure.

Because these precious moments are fleeting.

And things will be different a year from now.

HANDS FREE WEEKLY INTENTION

Remove Any Remaining Distraction Temptations

Perhaps the simplest yet most effective strategy I used to permanently abandon my highly distracted life was changing the notification settings on my phone. With the device in silent mode, my time and attention were not sabotaged each time I received an email, phone call, or text. Suddenly that temptation to "check" was no longer present. Rather than trying to multitask my attention in several directions, I was focused solely on the person in my company or on the activity at hand.

This week, protect time with loved ones by creating barriers between you and your distraction. For example:

- Remove the applications from your phone that most capture your time and attention.
- Turn off all notifications on your phone.
- Purchase an inexpensive digital camera or flip phone that does not have the capabilities of a more advanced device. Having your camera separate from your phone will reduce the temptation to use the phone for other purposes when you pull it out to take a photo.
- Place your phone in a drawer, on a shelf, or in the closet.
- Have your child create a phone sleeve or wrapper with paper and crayons to house your phone.
- Leave the phone in the car when you get home.
- Use a paper calendar instead of a digital one to discourage reaching for the phone or tablet.

Daily distractions have a sneaky way of stealing time — that rare and precious commodity that once we lose, we never regain. Every time we get online to check email, social media, or search the Internet, suddenly a large chunk of time disappears. Is that really how we want to spend our precious time? By removing the temptations of the phone and Internet, you will receive the gift of time — time to laugh, time to love, and time to live for what most matters in your life.

HANDS FREE REFLECTION

Gratefulness

Today I Lived

Today I was awakened by the sound of shuffling feet.

It was my early-bird riser in her big sister's pajamas that dragged across the floor.

I wanted to pull the covers over my head and feign sleep.

But instead I got up and made toaster waffles that she said tasted "divine."

She kissed me with syrupy sweet lips.

Getting up wasn't my first response. But I did it.

Today I lived.

Today she lost her shoes for the thirty-seventh time in two weeks.

It was right before we needed to head out the door.

I wanted to scream, to scold, to throw my hands in the air.

But instead I held her. I held her. My shoeless girl.

Together we found them wet with dew in the backyard and she whispered, "Sorry I am forgetful, Mama."

Being calm wasn't my first response. But I did it.

Today I lived.

Today the birds chirped noisily through the open back door.

Their cheerful chatter seemed to accentuate the deadlines, the laundry, the mess piled up around me.

I wanted to slam the door and silence the temptation; there was so much to do.

But instead I put on my running shoes and my favorite hat.

With each step, I got closer to what mattered and farther from what didn't.

Letting go wasn't my first response. But I did it.

Today I lived.

Today I stood in front of the mirror sizing myself up.
It was apparent that stress and lack of sleep had left their mark.
I wanted to dissect each wrinkle, pinch each layer of soft skin.
But instead I looked away and said, "Not today. Only love today."
Loving myself wasn't my first response. But I did it.
Today I lived.

Today I threw together a simple dinner and scooped it onto the plate.
It looked pathetic and unappealing.
I wanted to question my worthiness based on my culinary skills.
But instead I hollered, "Let's eat outside on the porch! Everything
tastes better outside."
Offering myself grace wasn't my first response. But I did it.
Today I lived.

Today I was on a mission to tuck my child into bed as quickly as
possible.
It had been a tiring day, and I just wanted to be alone.
She asked if she could listen to my heartbeat.
Reluctantly, I lay down beside her and she drew her head to my chest.
"We have the same heartbeat," she announced.
"How do you know?" I asked, expecting some childlike reasoning, but
instead her poignant response brought me to my knees.
"Because you are my mom."

And there it was. My confirmation.

To choose to stay when I want to retreat.
To choose to forgive when I want to condemn.
To choose to love when I want to attack.
To choose to hope when I want to doubt.
To choose to let go when I want to hang on.

To choose to stand when I want to fall.

Today I lived.
It wasn't my first response.
But I share the same heartbeat with two precious souls.
And that's enough to get me through the day.
I will choose to live again tomorrow.
And for that choice, I am grateful.

REFLECTION QUESTIONS

Think back to the way you lived before you began your Hands Free journey. How are you different now? How have the interactions with your family changed? How has the atmosphere of your home or your car changed?

Throughout your journey, did you experience feelings of confirmation that led you to believe you are on the right path? In what ways are you grasping what matters more than you did before?

What will be your biggest obstacle in staying committed to your Hands Free way of life? How might you combat that challenge?

CONCLUSION

I STILL HAVE THE SHOES—the shoes I was wearing on the day I broke down on the hot Tarmac of an Alabama hill when I honestly answered the question, "How *do* I do it all?"

The treads are now worn to the nub. The style is outdated. But I can't seem to part with them, my tear-stained shoes that became my dig-for-your-life shoes.

When I look at them, I remember myself crouched down in exhaustion, releasing my deepest, darkest fears into the atmosphere. With my head bent forward, the tears fell directly on my shoes. It struck me as odd that they should hit my laces and not the cement beneath me. Yet seeing my shoes as a target for my tears suddenly gave me a target for my life.

I knew I wanted out.

I knew I wanted less.

I knew I wanted more.

I wanted to grasp what mattered before my children accepted their high school diplomas and I didn't know them, *really* know them, at all.

I wanted to grasp what mattered before a tornado or other natural disaster took everything I owned, and I suddenly realized "things" don't really matter at all.

I wanted to grasp what mattered before the doctor whispered a prognosis that made me beg for a second opinion and plead to the heavens for a little more precious time.

I wanted to grasp what mattered before my heart realized my lungs had become "too busy" to breathe and I would surely die.

As I stared at my tear-stained shoes that pivotal day, I considered my options.

I could flop myself in the grass and simply give up. I could turn back toward home and accept my distracted life as just the way it was going to be. Or I could pray to God for guidance and strength in order to transform my distracted life.

When I felt God's comforting presence assuring me there was hope, I chose option three. I began running forward, and I didn't look back. That's when my tear-stained shoes became my dig-for-your-life shoes. That was the moment I began digging for air, digging for hope, digging for life.

Do you want to know something funny?

I planned to live Hands Free for one year. I thought after one year of *grasping what really mattered* I would be cured. I thought my life would then be permanently void of distraction. I thought I would be completely connected to what mattered and immune to distraction. I thought it would be easy to be fully present in each moment at hand.

Reading that now makes me laugh. Because my journey is far from over. My pursuit to live a Hands Free life will likely last forever.

Don't get me wrong; I am not slamming my progress, not in the least. In fact, I know with certainty that I have made significant progress in my battle against the daily distraction that prevents me from living a present and gratitude-filled life. But even if I were to become the most fully present, undistracted individual in the world, daily distraction would still come knocking on my door. Daily distraction will always be ready and willing to steal my Sunset Moments and sabotage my relationships.

Every single day, I am faced with choices on how I will spend my precious time. This includes large amounts of time: *Do I say yes to heading up a community event or use that time to do something I am truly passionate about?* This includes small amounts of time: *Do*

I quickly tuck my child into bed or spend ten minutes talking to her about her day? And this includes mere seconds of time: *Do I look up from my phone to greet my loved one or do I continue typing a text message?*

The choices I make matter.

The choices I make are critical.

The choices I make mean everything.

Because it is in the moments that I choose *what matters* over distraction that I make lasting connections and create priceless memories with the people I love. I realize there will come a day when those loving human connections and beautiful memories will be all I have left. So in the meantime, I choose to keep running ahead—running toward what really matters and not looking back.

There will never be a finish line. But there is something far better.

Every single time I let go of distraction to grasp what really matters, I am embracing life.

And life will embrace me back.

 HANDS FREE FINAL REFLECTION

In Your Honor*

In your honor, I will smile at the surly cashier. I will smile at those with no smile because I don't know what battle they're facing today.

In your honor, I will say yes to gumball machines and holding a big, fat toad that will probably pee on my hand. Because this makes my kids happy—and one day they will remember I said yes to gumballs and toads.

In your honor, I will take the stairs. I will take the scenic route. I will take a chance if it's something worth fighting for.

*In honor of Christy B., a faithful reader of my blog, who died from melanoma at age forty-three—but not before she grasped every precious moment of life that she possibly could.

In your honor, I will let that agitated driver into the line of traffic although I waited my turn. I will even wave and wish him well.

In your honor, I will celebrate the rare occasion when my child grabs my hand as we walk through a parking lot. And I will relish the unusual occurrence that she leaves her hand in mine far longer than necessary.

In your honor, I will buy the pretty undergarments on the same day I say, "Yes, I'll take extra hot fudge."

In your honor, I will pause for sunsets, goodbyes, and belly laughs. I will acknowledge such things are miracles. Everyday miracles.

In your honor, I will carry an extra dollar bill just in case I see that man on the corner of Clairmont and Thirtieth with a sign that says, "Can you spare some change?"

Because I always have a little hope to spare.

In your honor, I will schedule my mammogram and dermatologist appointments. And I will pester my friends to do the same.

In your honor, I will slide my hand beneath the covers until I find my husband's hand. Not for any reason, just because he's there . . . thank goodness, just because he's there.

In your honor, I will sing in the car. I will sing in the shower. Even though it sounds unpleasant. Even though I don't know the words. I will sing.

In your honor, I will say, "I am sorry." Even when it's difficult to say. Even when I think the other person should say it first.

In your honor, I will visit my kids in the lunchroom until they say, "No more, Mom. I am too old for that." And then I will periodically ask——just in case they change their mind and need me to come one day.

In your honor, I will stop prefacing sentences with "When I lose five pounds" and "When things slow down."

In your honor, I will live life now, not "someday."

In your honor, I will bless the butterfly that crosses my path. You taught me everyday miracles are abundant if we just open our eyes and look for them.

In your honor, I will not let life pass me by.

ACKNOWLEDGMENTS

I DIDN'T WALK THIS JOURNEY ALONE. My blog and this book exist only because of the many individuals who walked beside me and at times even carried me throughout this process. What really matters in my life looks like this ...

I will be forever grateful to the nine remarkable women who graciously read the first Hands Free stories ever written. The feedback I received from Beth Berutich, Shannon Brooks, Lori Fulk, Julia Griffith, Jennifer Harbour, Mary Largent, Stacie Oliver, Jamie Shaw, and Eleanor Williams gave me the courage to publish my stories on a blog. Their support has remained steady throughout this journey, and their love for my children and me is my daily fuel. As individuals, each of these women has played a vital role in my life and in this journey. I am forever indebted to each one.

To my dear friends who devotedly read and shared my blog posts, let me say this: Your name is, and forever will be, imprinted on my heart. Each time you forwarded my blog post to a friend, taped it up at the doctor's office, shared it with your child's soccer coach, and posted it to your Facebook wall, my readership grew a little more. Because of your unwavering support, *The Hands Free Revolution* is what it is today. A special word of thanks goes to my Liberty Crossings United Methodist Church family for their unwavering support and help in spreading the Hands Free message. Pastor Keith Elder and Pastor Wade Griffith offered words of encouragement that lifted me over many stumbling blocks and periods of self-doubt. I am truly grateful for the faithful backing of my friends through every step in my journey.

To the members of *The Hands Free Revolution* community, my loyal companions who I have come to know through your beautiful messages, it has been a privilege to share this journey with you. I have saved every encouraging word you have written to me. Your heartfelt stories were a continuous source of inspiration and hope, which is why many of them became a part of this book. You have been my greatest unexpected blessing of going public with my struggles and triumphs to grasp what really matters in life. The words, "You are not alone," took on a whole new meaning when you grasped my hand and walked beside me.

This Hands Free Mama was greatly inspired by the work of Brené Brown, Glennon Doyle Melton, and Patti Digh. Through the eloquent words of these brilliant women, I was inspired to live authentically, to be brave with my truths, and to stop waiting to live. My writing was also fueled by the music of Mat Kearney and Tristan Prettyman. Mat's lyrical masterpieces continually inspired my journey and played nonstop throughout the writing of this book. Tristan's healing voice, particularly the song "Come Clean," inspired greater introspection and candor throughout the editing process. Thank you, Mat and Tristan, for putting your stories to music so we can all feel a little less alone in our struggles to live and love.

Going from a blogger to a published author was a far-fetched dream until the day Laura Corn sent me an email that said, "Laura Corn is a fan." That's the day I saw a glimmer of hope that perhaps my stories were book-worthy. There is no greater gift to a writer than a loving and knowledgeable mentor. Laura has been that and more.

Without the ongoing technical assistance and extreme patience of Greg Fulk and Connie Brigham there would be no Hands Free Mama logo, no blog, and no medium for my stories to reach the world. I am grateful for their knowledge and expertise in navigating website issues, server crashes, and all things techy, because computer code is a language this creative writer will never be able to decipher. Connie and Greg gave my words a home and a light so others could find me. I will be forever grateful to both of them for such a priceless gift.

This book is a product of the encouragement and prayers I received from many individuals. Kellie McIntyre was a sounding board for my vision in the early stages of this process and provided valuable input on many aspects of the book. Michelle Belcher's encouragement came in the form of emails that began with, "Your blog post today reminds me of a country song …" Michelle is responsible for a wealth of motivational wisdom and for getting me on the bike to relieve the stress that comes from writing a large number of words in a very short time. Carron Rary read my blog posts religiously and provided words of wisdom and affirmation that only a seasoned mother could provide. Carron also loved both of my babies like her own as she prepared them to be successful in first grade—and in life. Kristin Shaw came across my blog in its infancy. She saw an initiative worth endorsing and she did, with every fiber of her being. As a fellow writer and blogger, Kristin became my confidant in times of frustration and doubt. On one particularly rough night, I considered deleting my blog. But instead, I sent a message to Kristin. Kristin's response inspired a profound revelation that forever ceased outside negativity from impeding my journey. Shannon Brooks played a critical role in bringing strength, calmness, and hope into my seasons of doubt. Shannon intuitively knew when I was empty and needed refueling. So many divine revelations to follow my heart and just keep writing came from Shannon's calming voice. Eleanor Williams was the first person with whom I shared my brutal truths. I knew she was a keeper when she didn't run as fast as she could in the other direction. In fact, she provided company for my painful truths by sharing her own. "When we see each other's scars, we love each other more" was something I wrote, and now live by each day, because of Eleanor.

On my publishing journey, Katie Mohr and Christi McGuire were my guiding lights. With great expertise and love, they helped me navigate the twists and turns of book proposal writing, query letters, and publishing. When my creativity was weighed down by the mechanics of writing, they lightened my load. When I came to a fork in the road, they helped me figure out the best route. Their support system and belief in me provided the courage and confidence to persevere until I reached my destination. When Katie and Christi read this book, I hope they see their golden touches that line every page.

The day Sandra Bishop called me was the day my dream took flight. Within minutes of talking to her, I knew with certainty that my *Hands Free Mama* manuscript had been waiting for her capable hands. Sandra far exceeded my expectations of a literary agent by working tirelessly to open up many incredible options for this book. Sandra is my confidant, my voice of reason, my bulldog, my rock star, and my cheerleader. Sandra is a blessing and a true gem. I will be forever indebted to Jill Savage, an inspiration and role model to me in so many ways, who provided the divine connection that led Sandra to me.

It was the voice of my editor, Carolyn McCready, that led me to choose Zondervan as the publisher of this book. She has the kind of voice that makes you open your heart because you know your secrets will be safe with her. She has the kind of voice that makes all your doubts and worries fade away. She has the kind of voice that makes you feel certain she came into your life for a reason. In Carolyn's loving and skillful hands, not only has this book grown, but I have also grown. Carolyn saw potential in both the book and in me and has lifted us to heights unimagined. Bob Hudson, my extraordinary copy editor, has a talent for seeing both the small details *and* the big picture, making this book what it is today. I am grateful to Bob for giving me grammatical freedom so my voice could remain true to who I am. Along with Carolyn, the entire Zondervan family has been extraordinary. I am especially grateful for the support and kindness extended to me by my publicists, Heather Adams and Beth Gebhard, as well as my marketing director, Londa Alderink. Their belief and passion for the Hands Free message is evident in their remarkable efforts to spread it to every corner of the world.

It's not often you marry a man and his family not only loves you like a daughter and a sister, but they become your biggest supporters and fans. To Patti, Bob, Stacie, Jon, and Brad, it secretly pleases me to know you discuss my latest blog posts while milling around the copy machine at work ... and that you keep a stack of *Reader's Digest* on your desk just in case someone hasn't seen my article ... and that you call from the parking lot to say you can't go into the office until you stop crying over today's blog post. I am especially grateful to my gorgeous nephews, Sam and Evan, for allowing me to relive the precious baby days without the stress and sleepless nights that go with them. I also thank my nephews for allowing Natalie and Avery to love them so much that they cry whenever we have to say goodbye.

My sister, Rebecca, was the one who bought me a how-to-blog book, and then she pestered me so much about starting a blog that it became quite annoying. In the first year of blogging, when challenges arose with naysayers, inner doubt, and low blog traffic numbers, Rebecca always had a supportively feisty word and a cool song to lift my spirits. Not only did my sister celebrate all my successes; she tweeted them to the world. Rebecca's editing skills came in handy if I wanted a *really* tough critique, so using my sister as an editor was short-lived, but appreciated all the same. Rebecca believed I had a message to deliver before I believed it myself. I can never thank her enough for that.

I am most grateful to my parents, Harry and Delpha, who have read and celebrated everything I ever wrote from the story-writing days in Miss Paluska's second-grade class to every single draft of this book. It has been my greatest prayer that they would live to see me publish a book. If I had a dollar for every time my mom said, "I just can't wait to hold your book in my hands," I could retire today and give the term "Hands Free" a whole new meaning. All my life, my parents have been the best listeners I have ever known. They have and always will be my favorite people to talk to about life. I want my parents to know that the reason I had the courage to share the difficult truths contained in this book was because of what they said to me when I was sixteen: "No matter what you do, no matter what mistakes you make, we will always love you." My parents kept their word by loving me through the good and the bad, and I promise to honor them by providing the same unconditional love for my daughters.

To Avery, my ukulele-playing songbird with smiling eyes: My life changed the day I started seeing life from your perspective. Through your eyes, there is beauty in panda 'jamas, in bright yellow dandelions, and in toothless smiles. You taught me that it is only when we slow down that we see all that is beautiful. Thank you for assuring me that we have time to listen to heartbeats and plant apple seeds in the backyard. Avery, it is you who put the joy on the pages of this book.

To Natalie, my brown-eyed beauty with an enormous heart: I learned what matters in life by watching you walk right up to the suffering and extend your hand. "Because when you have the important things in life—like love, faith, and family—there is nothing you own that you can't give away." I penned those words by watching you live. You taught me that combating the world's problems isn't that hard—you just start with a person who looks sad. Through years of nightly Talk Time, your voice articulated what really matters in life. The heart of this book belongs to you, Natalie.

To my husband, Scott: Without your support, my blog and this book would not be in existence. You are the sole reason I was able to take a leap of faith and attempt to do what I was born to do: be a writer. You believed in my vision of helping others let go of distraction and provided the tools, the Apple computers, and the tech support to make it happen. You have loved me at my worst and celebrated with me at my best. Thank you for being my number one fan. Your love and care for my health and well-being have added ten years to my life. What a privilege it will be to spend them with you.

Thank you, God, for guiding my feet and freeing my hands so I could find my way home.

CHARITABLE ORGANIZATIONS MENTIONED IN THE BOOK

Compassion International
12290 Voyager Parkway
Colorado Springs, CO 80921
Phone (800) 336-7676
www.compassion.com

Operation Christmas Child
Samaritan's Purse
P.O. Box 3000
Boone, NC 28607
Phone (828) 262-1980
www.samaritanspurse.org/what-we-do/operation-christmas-child/

Water for Life
75-5851 Kuakini Hwy #75
Kailua Kona, HI 96740
Phone (808) 989-3735
www.waterforlife.org

Share Your Thoughts

With the Author: Your comments will be forwarded to the author when you send them to *zauthor@zondervan.com*.

With Zondervan: Submit your review of this book by writing to *zreview@zondervan.com*.

Free Online Resources at
www.zondervan.com

Daily Bible Verses and Devotions: Enrich your life with daily Bible verses or devotions that help you start every morning focused on God. Visit www.zondervan.com/newsletters.

Free Email Publications: Sign up for newsletters on Christian living, academic resources, church ministry, fiction, children's resources, and more. Visit www.zondervan.com/newsletters.

Zondervan Bible Search: Find and compare Bible passages in a variety of translations at www.zondervanbiblesearch.com.

Other Benefits: Register to receive online benefits like coupons and special offers, or to participate in research.